Up and Down like a Dog at a Fair

Helen Crawford

Chapter 1

Atomic Mutton

Older women - beware - from the classics, not to mention the soaps, the women's magazines and the entire accumulated acknowledged truth that everyone knows, common sense in fact, we learn this simple fact: men simply aren't interested in women over forty. Past forty? Forget it, love. You're past your sell-by date, a high miler, mutton dressed as lamb, granny's oysters, a farcical yet sinister bunny boiler, snatch 22: tragic sub-fertile menopausal harridan with facial hair and warts. And hairy warts. In the dank, hideous winter of your life. With no spring in sight, not even a nasty dismal grey one, not ever. Male comedians will dress up as you, and everyone except you will think it is hilarious. You will want to cry. Just crawl away and die. Go on.

I used to believe that. How tragic I was! That was before this happened:

I'm going to begin my story, right here, jumping in, and you'll have to keep up with me a bit, because in many ways it's not the beginning, any more than this is the end, with the day I went to the bank, that April, the cruellest month, great poets know these things, and enquired innocently about the status of my account. It was definitely the end of one part of my life, so necessarily the beginning of something else. It was a joint account. We'd always had a joint account, since we were married straight out of university. When we were but children, I now realise, looking back. I knew there was a lot of money in there, a vast heap of money, because we had sold our huge old family-size house to cope with his various financial and emotional crises, put all our furniture into storage and were living in a tiny rented flat. Consequently the account was bulging with equity, big fat equity, to the tune of four hundred and forty thousand pounds. I'm not going to talk much about him, by the way, make your own mind up: you might have to read a bit between the lines; even thinking about him for any length of time can cause me to turn shiraz with rage. Not shiraz rose either, but the good old purple stuff.

What with the general financial crisis and the daughter about to do GCSEs (not to mention having been married for seventeen years, and so not particularly trying any more), I had not been in the habit of giving a lot of time to my appearance so was a bit dishevelled hair-wise as I wandered into the bank that morning, had no make-up on, and was wearing a tweed overcoat with large green checks from the Help the Aged shop, which it would have been over-generous to describe as vintage. I would say it was a lower middle-class, mid-sixties coat, as from my childhood I remember women wearing similar things clutching Silver Cross pram handles and lurking around the primary school gate at home time. A Moors murderer type of coat. You get the picture.

The cashier, who was a snotty blonde with completely the wrong shade of lipstick, a cruel pink which clashed with her complexion in a strangely hypnotic way, how these details remain engraved on my mind, handed me the slip of paper with the mini-statement on it.

"Twenty-eight pounds forty-three pee," she said in a voice which suggested she had been sent to elocution lessons at some formative stage in her life.

"What? Not four hundred thousand and something? Pounds? Er - some more noughts?" I flailed.

"It's written down there for you," she said kindly, clearly feeling that her job was hard enough without having to deal with care in the community customers with mental problems, and pointing at the final total with a long, bright pink fingernail. It matched the lipstick. No chips on her lacquer. She turned away and started to shuffle some papers in a way which suggested I should move on. There was a hesitation while my emotions considered their options.

"Oh well, thank you, you've been very helpful," I said, clearing my throat, which seemed to have seized up. I never forget my manners in a crisis. It gains me thinking time, as well as being a lot less tiring than shouting.

I went home in a bit of a daze. He was packing.

"Where are you going? What's going on?"

"You don't need to know that." He left. In my car.

My daughter and I looked at each other. She was crying. I tried to remember what I was supposed to do, and eventually thought about giving her a hug, even though frozen snow women don't give the most comforting hugs in the world.

"Mum," she said.

I didn't say anything. I was thinking, and this is a strange thing to do in a crisis, and a bit masculine possibly (I like to think I am in touch with my masculine side) but I was thinking how pretty she is. How very extraordinarily pretty, and, even more importantly, young. What lovely hair, what fabulous skin etc. How nice to be sixteen. She also has a wonderful figure and a great brain. I thought, at least I don't have to worry too much about her. She'll be alright. Even if her father is a selfish bastard. The wanker. What the hell was going on?

Her name is Nancy.

"Mum," said Nancy again.

"Yes darling," I said.

"Mum, what are we going to do?" My shoulder was a bit soggy with tears, but she was slowing down the sobbing now.

"It'll be fine," I said, "for a start I can go and buy a computer now, the mean sod wouldn't let me get one. Hoorah, we can surf the web. And things. All that."

"But we haven't got any money."

"I'm going to get a job," I said, "and I'll get all the money back off the mean sod, I mean your dad, and we'll get a house, and we'll go on holiday, you'll see." I hesitated. "Even to Disneyland, if you like - " (I had always hated theme parks, so this was very noble).

"It'll be fine. Trust me. We'll manage." I said all this with splendid and commendable calmness.

"But what if you can't?" she wailed, falling onto the sofa in a theatrical attitude of despair.

"Have I ever not done anything I said I was going to do?" I demanded.

She looked at me in a way which I decided to interpret as hopeful and tentatively confident. I'm not fantastic at reading facial expressions. Or determining people's motives. Often, when I'm watching one of those films that depends heavily on eyebrow acting and subtle glances at the floor, I start to be all at sea about what's going on and have to nudge my companions for enlightenment. This is not always as endearing as I imagine it to be.

"And anyway, I don't want to go to Disneyland any more." This was the death of innocence, then.

I went to bed and I spent a night of total rigid sleeplessness and frozen terror during which the only bright spot was that I could literally feel the fat deposits on my thighs being sucked off for emergency use, as my body went into stress meltdown. The only other time I had observed this physical phenomenon was just after I gave birth for the first time, and on day two the fat on my thighs transferred itself to my breasts, for milk production purposes. It was like one of those mediaeval miracles, where beautiful virginal would-be saints acquired beards or lost their breasts or otherwise became uglified in order to shake off an un-Christian suitor. Only in reverse. On that occasion I woke up in hospital and staggered to the bathroom, remembering as I went that I had just had a baby, and wondering, where the hell was it? But I was momentarily distracted by the sight, in the mirror, of the most enormous breasts in the world. Unfortunately it was a very fleeting miracle, and no-one else was there to witness it. Typical.

After thinking about this kind of stuff all night (it was very exhausting) I got up and walked into town to see the solicitors who had sold our house and ask them if they did divorces as well.

The solicitors were housed in a beautiful Georgian townhouse with fancy banisters and an elegant portico. I tried to appear nonchalant. The receptionist, who was a grey haired and respectable looking woman with an amber necklace looked at me in a manner which I can only describe as quizzical, since I don't know exactly what it means and I don't know what she meant by looking at me that way. Admittedly my hair had not improved overnight.

"We do have someone available," she said. "Please take a seat and wait." I sat down to wait. I waited for ages. The receptionist kept glancing at me as if I might do something wrong at any moment. I didn't dare touch the copies of Yorkshire Life and The Yorkshire Post which were neatly arranged on the side table. Eventually, when I had almost decided to go and pace up and down outside, where the receptionist couldn't see me, suddenly, to my right, a huge pair of mahogany double doors creaked open and there stood a tiny little white-haired man in a dark suit.

"Mrs Meansod?" he enquired. (Obviously that's not a real name).

"Are you a solicitor?"

"Do come in." I'm not sure if I was ever ushered before but surely this was ushering, as I was guided tenderly across the huge carpeted space. I was installed in a comfy chair and the tiny man got out a notebook and a fountain pen. He was sitting behind a desk so huge that almost all I could see of my miniature solicitor was a quiff of fluffy white hair and a pair of kindly eyes beneath eyebrows like albino bottle brushes.

"Do tell me all about it, Mrs Meansod," he said gently and professionally as he uncapped his pen, so I began.

"Well," I said, "he's cleaned the account out and gone, but I think I know where and I think I know where he's put the money, so if we could -"

"I'm sorry to interrupt," said my gentle interlocutor, "but if we could just start at the beginning. How long have you been married?"

"Oh. Sorry. Seventeen years."

"Children?"

"One. Well there was another one, but - there isn't now."

"And your child is how old?"

"Sixteen. A girl, Nancy. But can't we talk about the money - ?"

"All in good time, Mrs Meansod."

He waved his hand at me and wrote carefully in longhand with his lovely fountain pen, and I started to feel a tiny bit frustrated.

"And how old are you now?"

"Forty-five," I quavered. "Old and past it".

"Nonsense," said the solicitor, peering at me from under his fluffy white eyebrows, "you're still a young woman. And a very attractive one, too, if I may say so." At this I started to cry properly at the thought of how useless and faded his eyesight was, and he passed me his hanky, which was a nicely folded proper white cotton one, with his initials in the corner. It smelled of ironing. I cried some more. After a while I slackened off a bit, and he said,

"Does Mr Meansod have a job?"

"He's in computers, but he was made redundant a year ago. We just moved from a big house in a village up the dale to a flat in town," I sniffled.

"And do you work?"

"I was a classroom assistant at the local school - and I did bits and pieces at the pub when they had work, but it's too far away now. And he's taken the car. My car, actually. His company car had to go back."

"I see," said my solicitor, whose name I still didn't know, but his initials were B.W.W. according to his hanky, as he wrote everything down laboriously in his notebook. I craned to see his handwriting, which I imagined to be copperplate, or possibly endless Elizabethan squiggles.

"And Mr Meansod has removed the money from your joint account?"

"Yes, yes," I said, sitting forward eagerly in my chair now that we were cutting to the chase, "and I'm pretty sure I know where - "

"We'll come to that in a moment... now then, joint account, containing... how much money?"

"Four hundred and forty thousand and twenty-eight pounds and forty-three pee."

He wrote it down very slowly.

"And he removed?"

"Four hundred and forty thousand pounds," I said at dictation speed. I felt I was starting to get the hang of this law stuff.

"Three hundred and forty thousand pounds. Which was the equity from a property owned jointly by you both?"

"Yes!" I almost shouted. "He stole it!"

"No no. Jointly owned. Not theft. Not in the eyes of the law. Are there any other assets of the marriage?"

"He's got a pension fund."

"Any idea what it's worth?"

"Not the foggiest. He never told me anything about money, did all the accounts -"

"And so," he began.

"Yes. I think he's got another -" I went on impatiently, forgetting that I was not allowed to go racing ahead in the story.

"First I need to establish - have there been any other grounds for divorce? Did he ever strike you?"

There was pause.

"Well, yes, but it was ages ago, and to be fair I hit him first. And harder."

"That doesn't matter." He carried on writing for a while. Then he looked up and beamed at me in satisfaction.

"I think I can safely say we have grounds here for several divorces."

"I expect that's good," I said, very patiently, "but about this money. What if he leaves the country?" I was clutching the edge of the seat so hard that my knuckles were white with anxiety.

"Is he likely to do that?"

"Well, he's got his passport, but I think he's gone to stay at his mother's. She has a bungalow for her gardener and her housekeeper, and the last two just left. I didn't blame them. It can't be much of a life, running round after her. She's the most horrible old hag. She says she's hoping for some eastern Europeans, preferably Poles, or possibly asylum seekers at a pinch."

"Address?" I gave him the address.

"He's Down South?" He made it sound like another country, possibly on a different continent, or planet. "We'll have to send a private detective from down there to go round and serve an injunction on him."

"Will we? Gosh." I was both thrilled and appalled by this idea. Visions of sleuths in trenchcoats and trilbies stalked menacingly across my mind causing me to miss the next question.

"I'm sorry?"

"I said, you say you have some idea what he might have done with the money?"

"Yes," (finally!) "well, ages ago I noticed from the bank statement - this was when he was still working - that he was putting part of his salary into another account. So I had a bit of a go at him and then he said he was doing it for security or something but as I objected he wouldn't do it any more. But I didn't trust him. He was acting a bit funny even then. Paranoid. So I wrote down the account number in my address book. Here you are."

"Well done, Mrs Meansod," he beamed.

"Please call me Holly," I said. "I mean, really. Please. And my name is Field. I'm not going to use his name ever again."

"I'll call you Holly if you call me Basil," he twinkled.

I went thoughtfully home, pausing only to buy a packet of the cheapest available hair dye at the chemist's. Dubious Divorcee Red, it should have been called, only in defiance of the Trades Descriptions Act they called it something like Untamable Chestnut. I would stoop to conker. As I pushed through the crowds of employed people with money in their bank accounts, I asked myself if I had got the joke solicitor, the one who was retired really but they couldn't make him stay at home all day with his battleaxe wife, it would be cruelty to the elderly, so they gave him hopeless cases like mine. Maybe all firms of solicitors have one tucked away somewhere. But Basil seemed to be on my wavelength so I decided to give him a trial period before I put my foot down and insisted on a real solicitor who knew how to use a computer. Or at the very least knew what a computer was.

So, the next day I went to the job centre, which isn't in our town, our town is too nice and posh to have things like job centres. It was in the next town. I went on the bus, and for the first time noticed lots of things which I normally never see as I zoom by with my eyes fixed on the road and errant drivers thereon. I noticed a heron by the river bank, its chin tucked firmly into its collar as it gazed gloomily at the cold brown soupy river Wharfe. And what I at first took to be gaily coloured flags along the bank turned out to be fertilizer bags, washed downstream in the flood waters and festooned among the branches of trees. How curious, I thought.

The job centre was in a sturdy concrete building which would appeal to all fans of Stalin's apartment blocks in Moscow, being minimalist without in any way aspiring to decadent chic. Inside they had made a bit of an effort with the décor since I last signed on as a student in the seventies. They had got rid of the bulletproof booths for a start. The staff tried to smile and look friendly, but failed. They presumably had some sort of cheerfulness performance target to meet. I looked at all the jobs, which were on little cards on the wall, as I shuffled round the room with the rest of the losers as if we were at a particularly absorbing and popular exhibition of rare artefacts at the V and A. There seemed to be a lot of demand for forklift truck operatives. Then I went and spoke to the young man at the desk. He had one of those little circular plasters on his neck which threatened to absorb my entire attention. I wondered if he had a spot. I had ditched the coat, the weather was a bit warmer, relatively speaking, and was wearing my only suit, which was navy blue with shoulder pads. I had last worn it in the eighties.

"Do you have any qualifications?" he asked.

"Well, I have a degree in English and French. Only I got it over twenty years ago."

"Hmmm. I don't really mean that kind of thing. I mean employment related skills. Computer literate?"

"Oh yes," I said. They had computers at the school where I had worked, and I had often marvelled at the ease with which even tiny children used them. And I could read what they wrote over their shoulders. So I'm sure that should count.

"Spreadsheets? Microsoft Project? Any certificates? Any NVQs? Any experience?" It was hopeless. He looked at me with what I took to be shuddering contempt. But I could have been wrong, perhaps he was cold. Or coming down off drugs and booze. Lucky him.

"We don't have anything to suit you this week. Come back in a few days, we might have some more."

I bought the local paper, I went to agencies, I asked everyone I knew, I went round looking in shop windows for cards, but no-one had any jobs for a middle-aged woman with untameable chestnut hair.

I went home to Nancy. Thank God for Nancy. I had to keep everything on track for her. Focus. My wonderful beautiful daughter. She was sitting at the dining table in a pool of golden light from the downlighter. Her hair hung about her face gleaming with the natural colour of youth. She was studying Hamlet for her exams and marked her place in the book before she stood up to give me a hug.

"How d'it go, mum?"

"Getting there, getting there. Need to go back in a couple of days, they think they'll have something for me."

"That sounds good, really good, mum."

"Yes."

"We need some more food. There's nothing for tea. Have we got enough money?" We walked to Tesco's and spent a long time examining everything carefully. I had never before read the backs of labels and the prices of everything with such attention.

"What about eggs? They're both cheap and nutritious."

"We can't get the cheap eggs, mum, they're from tortured concentration camp hens!" shrieked Nancy, so loudly that other customers looked at us in alarm.

"I wasn't going to get them, I was just looking - which ones can we get then?"

"I don't suppose we can afford organic?"

"Not unless it's the same price as tortured. Free range is probably the best we can do. Maybe we don't have to have eggs. What about bacon?"

"Ugh, we can't eat tortured pigs! Don't you know what they do to pigs? I saw a programme. They keep them in these evil pens, and the piglets can't reach their mothers properly, it's so sad, sometimes they die of loneliness, I can't even bear to think about it -"

I could see that Nancy was about to cry, so I hastily took her to the sweetie aisle and bought a bar of very good value chocolate. Fortunately this did the trick. I can only hope that no innocent chocolate growers suffered during its production. We bought a lot of stuff in the good value range, and from the marked down section. Good old supermarket. It occurred to me that they probably had excellent rubbish bins, if we got desperate. But even as it was we got a whole week's worth of meals for eight pounds ninety eight. One of the meals we planned was mushy peas and value luncheon meat, and another was value sardines on toast. Very sound nutritionally. Vitamins and omega three and everything. Value sardines were only nineteen pee! I never knew that before. We also got a bag of apples which had been reduced to ten pee for quick sale. Only one of them was really squashy. It was very satisfactory.

My next appointment with Basil, on the other hand, was less than I had hoped for.

"The private investigator is getting nowhere with serving the papers. Mr Meansod is simply not answering the door. He's tried three times now."

"But what can we do?" I panicked. "I have to feed my daughter," I added melodramatically. But frankly the whole business felt like a village hall production of a nineteenth century novel on acid. I couldn't remember exactly which one. One where the heroine is cast out and wanders around on the moors in very thin and unsuitable shoes. I was beginning to lose my already tenuous grip on reality.

"Fear not," said Basil like the angel Gabriel. "For behold -" He didn't really say behold. He said something about other mechanisms and getting hold of the money early next week, with which I had to be content, even though I hadn't really listened to most of what he was saying because I was having visions of Nancy as the little match girl, gazing through the windows of the rich at their sumptuous feasting, and freezing to death on the pavement.

When I got home she had eaten all the sardines, and only looked half guilty.

"I thought you might have eaten already? Because you were late. Whoops."

"It's fine, I'll just have toast."

"Oh. Sorry. I had all the bread too."

"But that was supposed to last a week!"

"I'm sorry, I was hungry."

I was losing weight rapidly what with all the stress and emergency fat use, and Nancy eating all the food; and trying on some old clothes that evening I discovered to my great delight that I fitted into my favourite dress, which had been sulking at the back of the wardrobe ever since I embraced the "anything goes in the country" philosophy of our village up the dale. For years the only thing I had asked of a garment was that it either washed, or sponged down well. I twirled about a bit in the frock and Nancy got a bit irritated after a while, which is rare for Nancy.

"What are you doing, mum? I'm trying to concentrate on my revision! It's very important you know. You do want me to get good GCSEs, don't you?"

"Of course I do, darling. Hamlet, isn't it? I can help you with that, I have some ideas. You know what?" I said, "I think Gertrude gets a really hard time. I mean, she's a woman of a certain age, she probably thinks she's done quite well to get Claudius, I bet there are loads of buxom wenches hanging round the Danish court, of course she needs a bit of make-up."

"Yes, thank you for the literary insight. But what's with the prancing around?"

"I'm thinking about advertising."

"What?"

"In the paper. You know. Desperate old woman seeks desperate old man, that kind of thing. A bit like Gertrude and Claudius really."

"You can't! How awful! What if someone found out!"

"Like who? No-one will find out. I think I need a man to distract me. Like falling off a horse and needing to get on one again. Besides, if I get taken out to dinner I won't need to worry about you scoffing all the nosh."

"Honestly, mother," Nancy said scornfully, "your vocabulary is pure Beano."

"It's my ideolect, darling, as I believe you once informed me. I always said you had far too much education for a girl."

Nancy threw Hamlet at me.

"I have excellent news, Mrs Meansod," said Basil on the phone.

"Holly," I said.

"Holly, yes. Mr Meansod has got himself a solicitor, and is prepared to discuss arrangements with us."

"Oh?"

"Because he's been to his bank and found that he's got an injunction on his account," said Basil with more than just a note of triumph, more like a trumpet voluntary of triumph. Even I could tell. I could see that, once Basil was roused, he would defend his lady to the death. And that lady, or rather woman, was me. Hoorah!

"Aha! So he can't get any money? He won't like that."

"He doesn't. And thus the communication channels are cleared."

"So, can I have some money yet?"

"Um - I'm sure I could lend you some if it's an emergency," Basil said, sounding a bit hurt, I suspected. I suppose he expected me to congratulate him a bit more effusively.

"No, no, I'll be fine, we need to go through the proper, er, channels, don't we."

"I promise I will expedite a transfer of funds early next week."

Next week! I thought but managed not to exclaim. We were down to twenty pounds and running low on food four days earlier than planned (I never noticed before how greedy Nancy was) but I spent some of it on bus fare back to the job centre. It proved to be a sound investment.

"Did you say you can speak French?" asked the youth with the plaster, almost bounding over to me as I stood gloomily by an advert for an enthusiastic, energetic and numerate assistant with a working knowledge of Excel, whatever that might mean. It sounded a bit deviant to me.

The young man was excited on my behalf. He beamed. I hoped someone was watching him that day, otherwise it would be wasted on the performance indicators. Interestingly, he had a different plaster but in the same place, now it was one of those blue ones you have in kitchens. I wondered if he moonlighted as a chef. Of course there could be any number of explanations.

"Do I!" I exclaimed over-eagerly, "I have a degree in it! Well, half a degree," I added rather unnecessarily. Luckily he didn't notice that I hadn't answered the question.

"Well," he went on encouragingly, "all you have to do is ring this number, have a conversation with them in French, and the job's yours." He pointed me towards one of the cards I hadn't reached yet.

"What job?" I read the card. It said: Call Centre requires French speaker, native preferred, as soon as possible. Call Martine on 01756 777111.

"You can ring from here, it's free," said the young man, who now took on an entirely different appearance and seemed to be bathed in a heavenly light, like an angel of a somewhat lesser, spottier order than the usual ones. I sensed that my sanity was once again on the edge.

"And they're desperate," he added.

"I must just go the loo, first," I quavered. In the ladies I ran through what French I could recall, talking to myself in the mirror. I was a bit pale. Je suis I am a pot of jam, tu es thou art a clot, il est, elle est, um, nous avons, vous avez... esèce de con, as I was taught to say while on the French exchange, café au lait... baise moi vite - none of this was going to be any use. I could have written them a very good essay on Sartre. Or indeed Montaigne, my very favourite French philosopher. Trouble was, when I did my degree the emphasis was more on lit than lang. I thought of the little match girl, wolfing down mushy peas and luncheon meat while trying to decide if Hamlet was gay, and if so, whether it all was his mother's fault as usual. I took a deep breath and made my way to the unsavoury grey phone booth, stained by a million despairing exhalations.

"Martine? This is Holly Field."

"Ici Holly Field."

"No, I mean - oh I see, I mean yes, I mean oui, sorry, I mean ici Holly Field. Bonjour." I laughed in what I hoped was a jolly way but probably sounded hysterical.

"Vous telephonez pour la position?"

"Oui," I said confidently.

"Vous parlez bien français alors?"

"Oui, je parle bien," This was going surprisingly well.

"Dites-moi, alors," said the annoying French woman, "pourquoi vous voulez travailler ici?"

"Um, er, parce-que j'ai une fille qui a quinze ans qui s'appelle Nancy et elle mange beaucoup de - de poisson, er, sardines: vous savez? Comment est-ce que on dit ça en français? C'est probablement sardines n'est-ce pas? - et je n'ai pas d'argent. Parce-que mon mari est disparu," I added finally. I was rather pleased with this burst of French, produced by pure adrenaline.

"I don't understand," she said, sounding just as annoying in English. I don't know why, I thought, I'm speaking your bleeding language.

"Do you have experience of this work?" I thought of the pub.

"Well, I have worked answering the phone, and -"

"En français, s'il vous plait."

"J'ai travaillé avec un telephone, oui, et j'ai parlé aux gens qui ont besoin d'information" I said triumphantly, feeling fairly sure I'd said I helped people to find information, which I did when they rang the pub about opening hours and stuff, but Martine was tutting ominously. There was a long silence, and I wondered if she had put the phone down on me. Then she sighed.

"We need someone urgently," she said after a pause. "Can you start tomorrow morning at eight-thirty please?"

Yes! Oui! I had a job! Nancy was very proud of me when I told her.

"I'm sorry I ate all the value luncheon meat," she said, "but I saved you some peas. I wasn't sure when you were coming back."

"No matter," I said, "tomorrow we go to the supermarket and buy whatever we like, up to the value of fifteen whole pounds."

"Hoorah!" Nancy shouted. We danced around the kitchen in our joy.

"Can we get prawns?" Nancy panted, still dancing.

"Of course," I said as I did a rather complicated and indescribable dance move round the cooker. "Cheap ones. Value prawns."

"And baking potatoes? What about sausages? Tomato sauce? But it has to be Heinz. I'm not having value tomato sauce."

"Why the hell not? Let's go mad! But it has to last until I get paid."

"When do you get paid?" Nancy was doing a passable imitation of a pole dancer in the doorway.

"I'm not sure." We stopped dancing.

"People are giving me their sandwiches at school, because they feel sorry for me," Nancy said sadly. We hugged, and I sniffed the back of her neck, which smelled of child.

"I love you, child," I said.

"I love you, mum," she said.

Chapter 2

Mr Happy's business suit

In spite of what Nancy thought about it, I was determined to put an advert in the paper. It was one of several inclinations I had at that time to do things which were rather out of character. I believe I was acting at a deeply instinctive level. Take note, any old women out there. I wanted to get a dog, for instance, even though I don't particularly like dogs. In fact they scare me very much. Especially big black ones which bark a lot. I believe I was traumatised as a child. But - in spite of or possibly because of this - I wanted to train this imaginary dog to bark at strangers, and take chunks out of them at my command. And I started to buy lottery tickets, something I'd never done before. These things seemed, at that stage of my life, to be the only thing to do. Inevitable, like having a temperature when you are ill. I was feverish with despair. What could I do? Get a dog and win the lottery of course.

I sat at the dining table in my dressing gown with a cup of tea after Nancy had gone to bed and composed an advert. It took quite a while, because I was trying to avoid the clichés that other advertisers seemed not to realise they were falling into. Most of them, for example, said they were either slim or bubbly, and occasionally, both, even though I had become convinced that bubbly was a euphemism for fat. Or possibly large-breasted. Which would make sense.

In the end, this is what my advert said:

Untameable chestnut woman, likes eating and dancing, not always in that order, seeks man with sexy shoes for whatever.

I have actually always liked men's shoes, but I have particular tastes - I like certain kinds of boots as long as they're not too girly, I like well polished brogues (especially brown ones, thanks to a formative experience on a French exchange when I developed a massive crush with my fellow exchanger's papa), I don't like slip-on shoes or sandals except under certain circumstances. Like being on a beach holiday. Or in a tropical clime. Men and their feet - it's a very important and somewhat neglected area. I could place the advert for free, but would have to run up my phone bill to pick up the replies. That was a bridge to cross later. Once my call centre earnings started coming in, I expected to be able to pay for little luxuries like phone bills again.

The day I started work was bright and sunny and from my new wardrobe of old clothes that I hadn't been able to wear for ages because I had been too fat, I found a nice skirt and a tee shirt and a lovely wool unstructured jacket that I hadn't worn for at least ten years, but was miraculously back in fashion. The call centre was on an industrial estate on the edge of the town with the job centre. I will call it Milltown. Everyone else who worked there seemed to be in their mid-twenties and they were all wearing dark suits. Martine came to meet me in reception, where I was sitting marvelling at the stream of clones coming through the door.

Martine was, as I had suspected from her voice, in her early thirties and frighteningly smart. Her hair looked as if it had been painted onto her head, and her suit was a size six. She had no hips at all, just a kind of swivel arrangement at the junction of impeccable jacket and pencil skirt. She looked askance at the untameable chestnut, then moved on to the ensemble, which her gaze went up and down twice. I couldn't tell if this was good or not. I was soon put right.

"We dress down on Fridays, when you can be so casual as you are today, but as this is your first day I will ignore. Please read this sheet, it tells you about the product, please learn the details, and then in 'alf an hour I will return and you will start work. You may get a coffee from the machine, it is twenty pence. It does not give change."

I looked at the sheet. It was all about computer monitors, a subject about which I knew nothing. Let's face it, like Basil, I barely knew what a computer was. My heart pounded anxiously. Was I supposed to be an expert? I got up to pace around in fear and for the first time noticed that I was not alone. Round the corner by the coffee machine sat a fat man in a brightly patterned sweater studying a sheet just like mine.

"Oh hello - snap!" I said, in what I hoped was a friendly way, holding out my sheet.

"I am sorry?" he frowned. His accent was thick and Northern European.

"Oh, I'm sorry, my name is Holly, I couldn't help noticing that you have the same sheet of instructions as me?"

"I? Oh yes. The monitors. I am Henk. I am doing the Dutch."

"Dutch? I thought it was French?"

"No, it is a pan-European campaign. They always call me in to do the Dutch. You are to do the French? But you are not French? They prefer the native speakers I think."

"I think they were a bit short of native speakers." Henk looked contemptuous. "But please," I went on, "can you tell me what this is about? I don't know anyth - that is, very much - about - these, um, particular, monitors."

"Oh it is not so difficult I think you do not need to know everything. If the clients have other questions you ask them to call another number. You just have to talk them through the script."

"The script?"

"You will see. It is very simple really. Very very simple. Insanely simple. A child could do it I think. Even a very stupid child." Alright, alright, of course a child could do it, I thought crossly, they're all using computers in their playpens.

"Why aren't you wearing a suit?" I asked

"I never wear a suit," he scowled, "they take me or leave me. Let them find another Dutchman in this creppy place."

Martine reappeared just as I had got a coffee and settled down again to study my sheet.

"Have you finished," she said, and it didn't seem to be a question. Henk and I stood up and followed her upstairs to the room where the calls were made. There were rows of desks, and at every desk a different language was being spoken, as this tower of Babel disseminated the word of monitor improvement to the rest of Europe.

"You will sit here," said Martine as she gestured to me to sit near the front. It felt like school. Henk went to sit near the back.

"Bye, Henk," I said but he did not reply.

I sat down. The people sitting near me smiled briefly and then went back to their conversations with their headsets. I had Swedish to the left and Italian to the right. Swedish was a rather attractive blond man in a blue shirt. Italian was a tiny little woman with giant breasts (bubbly) and enormous earrings like saucers on the side of her miniature head. I put on my headset, and looked nervously at my computer.

"It turns on - like this," said the attractive Swede as he broke off from what he was doing to reach over and push my button. I blushed.

"Oh, I knew that," I said, "I was just - checking that it's like the machine I'm used to." What - a typewriter?

Martine's voice suddenly barked in my headphones.

"Is there a problem? You 'ave not started?" She was sitting at a raised desk at the front of the room (between me and the door, I couldn't help noticing, in case I needed to make a run for it), and now I realised that she could listen in to any of us at any time.

"Just getting settled," I said.

"Well you must not spend too much time "settling". Your call rate must be at least thirty per minute."

"Thirty!" But Martine was gone, telling off the Germans instead of me.

A name had popped up on my screen, a number to dial, and below that, a list of questions was beginning to unscroll itself. I dialled the number.

"Monsieur Normand? Bonjour. Je me presente..." It was actually very straightforward as long as they didn't start wandering off message. I just had to read the questions out loud, and select, from a list, into which category their reply fell.

a) Has no interest whatever - b) already owns one - c) prefers another make - d) did not reply.

Soon, however, I began to run into complications. It could have come under the category

e) chats you up.

"Alors - vous est anglaise? You are English? Do you ever come to France? You are blonde, yes, with blue eyes? You will come to Bourgogne and I will buy you dinner..."

"Holly!" It was Martine again. "You must not waste time talking about things which are not in the script!"

"Sorry, Martine, they just witter on and I can't stop them."

"Witter? You do not even speak English." said Martine contemptuously. "Please stay in the script. You may have a ten minute, only, break at ten-sirty."

"Pssst" came a theatrical whisper from my right. It was the tiny Italian woman.

"Hello," I whispered. It was like being at school.

"Come outside with me for a smoke," she said.

"But I don't smoke."

"I know you don't. Nor do I."

At half past ten we cast off our headsets and headed for the door, where my new friend lit up a small cigar in an amber holder.

"I gave up cigarettes," she explained. "I don't smoke any more. Not since a month, now. My name is Carla. What is yours?"

"I'm Holly." She blew out a long, thoughtful cloud of smoke which made me cough slightly. She waved her hand as if she was thereby banishing my cough demons.

"Tell me about yourself, Holly."

"Not much to tell. I'm getting divorced. Earning some money." Carla pulled my arm to indicate intimacy.

"Do not - I warn you - get involved with any of the men here. They are charming - yes some of them - but they are all with baggage of a big kind."

"Like trunks?" I said as a joke but immediately regretted it.

"You know - big luggage. Oh alright."

"I am trying to help you. Believe me I speak from experience. I have been here a long time - far too long a time. This is how I know about the baggages."

"Thank you, Carla. I'm sorry, I always make stupid jokes when I'm nervous. I'm really nervous about all this."

I meant it, actually. I could see that in my newly single state I was going to be attracted to practically anyone, and sitting next to Anders, the Swede, was already beginning to make me tingle in unaccustomed ways. Well unaccustomed for a while, anyway. He was seriously attractive in that strong reliable Scandinavian way and that blue shirt. Also he smelt nice whenever he leaned over to press the odd button that I had mysteriously misplaced. And then when he smiled his (blue, same colour as his shirt) eyes kind of crinkled at the edges... he was bloody sexy. So yes, I could see why Carla was concerned.

"What's wrong with Anders?" I asked.

"Oh, nothing is wrong with Anders. Anders is practically perfect. And Mrs Anders thinks so too."

"I see. He doesn't wear a wedding ring."

"I think he puts it back on while he is driving home. If you look closely I believe you can see a faint white mark where it should be."

There was a silence for a while, and Carla smoked the stub of her cigar while I looked at the car park, and the hills beyond.

"Would you like to go out for a drink one time, Holly?" Carla asked, meeting my eyes with an expression that meant absolutely nothing to me. I began to suspect I had some disorder on the autistic spectrum. Why didn't I understand facial expressions? I hoped she didn't fancy me or something.

"That would be lovely," I said.

The pub Carla chose to go to on Saturday night was also in Milltown, as she lived there. I think I mentioned before that it's a bit rough. It was the first time I had been out in a pub on a Saturday night for a very long time and I was a bit intimidated by some of the customers.

There was a terrace at the back where lots of people were smoking under patio heaters. This was where the crush was greatest. The place was packed solid. There seemed to be a fashion for men to have alarmingly short haircuts. This made them look aggressive and not very clever, a look which for some reason they imagined made them attractive to women. The women on the other hand were wearing hardly any clothes. I felt the women had thought out their strategy more carefully than the men. But then what would I know? The last time I dated anyone was in the eighties, as I had met Nancy's father in my first week at university. Since then I had had the odd mild crush, usually on the father of one or the other of Nancy's friends, and that had been the sum total of my romantic life. So I gazed with interest at the courtship rituals around me. And I didn't like the look of it.

Carla seemed quite relaxed as she downed a large glass of wine in about three gulps. She was wearing a lovely, navy blue jersey dress and black boots with a different but still enormous pair of saucer earrings. They looked as if they would pick up satellite signals from distant galaxies. I still couldn't work out how old she was.

"How old are you Carla?" I asked.

"Fifty-three, darling, what did you guess?"

"I thought a bit younger than me. Late thirties, possibly"

"Oh, how sweet of you to say so. No, I am very old indeed. I have had a long and crazy life."

"Tell me," I said.

"Oh, what is there to tell? I'm sure you can guess at most of it. Was I married? Yes, but no more. No children, thank the good God. With my husband I was living for many years in East Africa, in Tanzania, do you know where that is?"

"Not the faintest idea."

"On the right hand side, about half way down."

"Right. That helps."

" - running a safari lodge, I once wrestled a hyena off him in the bar, it had scented the leftover salami, but owing to their unfair divorce laws I got nothing when I left him. I am still fighting for my share of the property. They say I wasn't properly married in the first place. Male chauvinist bastards."

"Why did you come to England? Why not go back to Italy?"

"Ah, that is another story. Do you want another? I need another glass of wine."

She pushed her way through the shaven thugs to get to the bar. I noticed a short but attractive man (with actual hair) looking wistfully after her as she went. At least I think it was wistful. It could have been that he was a hitman, hired by her ex-husband in Tanzania and the thoughtful look in his eyes was because he was plotting how to take her out without detection. When Carla came back with two more enormous glasses of wine I asked her if she recognised the man who had been watching her.

"What man?" she asked, looking around

"Over there," I pointed, but he had gone. "Well he was over there."

"Describe him exactly."

"Um, short, brown hair, stocky -"

"You mean fat?"

"No, just not thin. Green shirt, brown jacket. Nice eyebrows."

"Nice?"

"Expressive. Not that I would know what they were expressing."

"What do you mean?" demanded Carla. I explained about my inability to read facial expressions and body language.

"You know, you read all these things in magazines about what it means if people are rubbing their noses and so on."

"Noses are very dubious darling. But seriously, you don't need to worry about exactly what it means. It's not a list, it's communication on the subconscious plane. You don't read it, you feel it. Use your instincts and feel when someone is going to love you or hurt you. And stop reading those magazines."

"So what do noses mean?"

"It's him rubbing his substitute for his penis while he thinks of you. Or so they say. I believe. But maybe he has an itchy nose."

"Oh. So what if I do it, what does that mean?"

"It means you are very mixed up and peculiar, but of course we knew that already, just looking at your hair."

"Well, it was grey before. The shock made it worse."

"Shall we go to another pub, when you've finished that one?"

Although I getting a bit tipsy by now I was happy to stagger out on to the cobbles and be led through an alley and a snicket and another alley (which smelt quite strongly and unpleasantly of wee) and out on to a path by the canal. There was another pub by the canal. It was charming. It was quite different from the last one. There was no music and no naked skin on view, apart from hands and faces, obviously. Instead, middle-class couples sat at tables drinking real ale and nice wine. There was a real fire. When we asked for glasses of wine we were given a menu to choose from. Carla couldn't read it without her glasses.

"Can't I just have a glass of dry white wine, is it too much trouble?" she demanded.

"We'll have two glasses of the Sauvignon Blanc," I said hastily. The waitress looked confused.

"That one." I pointed.

"Oh, the Sauvignon Blanc," she said reproachfully, as if it was my pronunciation which was faulty. Cheek! I may not know a lot of French, but I certainly know how to pronounce it.

Chapter 2. Mr Happy's Business Suit

The wine tasted no better than it had in the previous pub, but came in mercifully smaller glasses. Carla looked at hers disapprovingly.

"It is lucky for you that you met me now," she said. "I can teach you a lot about life as a single woman. There are so many traps to fall into. Men, I am sorry to say, are mostly bastards."

"Oh, not really."

"Oh they don't mean to be. They mean to be nice, but they can't help being bastards. They try so hard to be good, it is pathetic, but their true natures always shine through."

"Not all of them, surely!"

"I hope you may live to prove me wrong, darling," Carla said, knocking back her glass of wine in one. She did not appear to be even slightly drunk, while I was beginning to feel distinctly ill.

"I must just go to the loo," I said. I was so glad to be sick in the nice clean middle-class pub where I had the ladies to myself (apart from a woman in glasses and a Rohan jacket who got out quickly when she heard me retching). Imagine if I had been surrounded by nymphets in tiny stretchy garments re-applying their glitter. Like Bottom surrounded by pitying but merciless fairies.

When I got out, Carla was nowhere to be seen. After hunting round a bit I asked the bar staff if they'd seen her.

"Went out for a smoke, she said," said the girl who knew no French.

I saw her on the footbridge over the canal. As she inhaled, the red glow of her cigar was briefly reflected in the dark canal. Then I heard the hiss as the butt hit the water. I thought I could see another person on the bridge, but it was so dark by now that I couldn't be sure. By the time I got there Carla was alone.

"I think we should get you home," she said, taking my arm. We got each other to the bus station. Carla was walking back to her house in Milltown, but I was getting the bus back to Morton Spa. For the first time that evening, I wondered if Nancy was worrying about me.

Carla gave me a hug at the bus stop.

"I will see you on Monday," she said. "Take care."

"And the same to you," I said, climbing aboard the double decker.

It was a horrible journey home. Nothing to see out of the windows as it was dark, really unpleasant people doing things I did my best to avoid seeing in every corner of the bus, eventually I went and sat as near to the driver as possible and chatted nervously to him all the way home.

"So, are you finished for the night after this?"

"Yes I bloody am, and this is your stop," he said as he braked a little over-vigorously, sending the weirdos flying.

I got off. I went home to Nancy. She was sitting at the table, revising. The dear beloved girl. How was it possible for anyone to be so good? I thought of myself at her age, and had fleeting pangs of doubt. What if this calm exterior was a fake? Of course I had been a terrible daughter, but Nancy was so cool, and self-confident, and sensible. Goodness, I was lucky to have a daughter like that. But of course, I was a much better mother than my mother had been.

Mothers eh? What a job to take on. Nothing you ever do is right. (Unless, like me, you're blessed with a perfect daughter like Nancy). Now, you may be wondering: speaking of mothers, why my mother has not yet made an appearance? Surely one's family would rally round one at a time like this? Well, there's a simple explanation. My family was miles away, down South, and all incredibly busy. My mother and father are divorced, and have an unofficial competition for the most glamorous lifestyle award. My mother has bridge nights nearly every weekday, and goes to the theatre and/or a musical soiree every weekend. She stomps fiercely along her local bridleways making sure they are kept clear for ramblers, (swishing venomously at the nettles and brambles with her stick) and attends a book club where she regularly prepares papers for the edification of her fellow clubbers. "I've written this paper on Larkin, I'll read you a bit," she will say on the phone, before launching into a massive tract on what love is all about. She also goes on holiday at least three times a year, and my sudden marriage rupture happened to coincide with the long-awaited Himalayan trek she had been planning ever since her Katmandu trip.

"It was lovely, you know, but I need to get off the beaten track and away from all those tourists. It was a bit tacky you know, not what you want. But my friend Bronwen said this trip was much more select. Trekking in a part of Nepal that has been closed until recently. Bronwen and I will be a bit of a revelation, ha ha! Only thing is, the insurance people kicked up a fuss about my arthritis! I had to get a letter from Dr Taylor to persuade them to let me go. Ridiculous. Anyway I go on the fourth for three weeks and if I don't come back in a body bag you can expect a long email about my trip! Ha ha ha!"

She's seventy-four.

My dad was in his house in France:

"This is Donald. I'm not here at the moment, but if you want to leave a message (unidentified shrieky noise) - what the hell - beeeeep"

My sister was run off her feet.

"Hello Jane? How are you?"

"I can't talk to you long, we've got violin class in fifteen minutes and Dougie hasn't done any practice, so he's doing it now" (that's why she was shouting, I could hear the dear boy sawing away in the background) "plus Max has a birthday party to go to and I'm just trying to find a suitable present for a seven year old boy - this is stuff I have in stock, let me run them by you: a soil testing kit (I got it from the eco catalogue), a super water pistol from the Woolworth's sale, a bean sprouter or one of those woolly hats boys like?"

"The gun. Or possibly the hat," I said firmly.

"But his parents are very right on," she wailed, "what if they don't approve?"

"You still can't go wrong with the hat," I pointed out, "but is the present for the child or the parents? And what are you doing with a stock of presents anyway?"

"I get them in the sales. I think the bean sprouter." Well, good, a decision.

"I'm sorry, I have to go, Charlie has just emptied his potty into the fish tank..." The line went dead.

So really it was just me and Nancy. I took her with me when I went to see Basil at the end of the week. He was charmed and delighted by her, and spent several minutes burying us in our chairs in the waiting room under a blizzard of compliments. Eventually I followed him through to the office and he told me that he had not got any money for me yet, he was pleased about the job, and that I had to go to court and swear on the bible that everything I had said was true.

"On the bible!"

"I'm afraid so."

"It's like voodoo. They'll be asking me to recite the Lord's prayer backwards next."

"The sooner it gets done, the sooner we can get the divorce over and then you can get on with the rest of your life," Basil pointed out. Nancy and I had to rush off as we were en route to parents' evening via a skip I had observed from the bus and felt merited investigation.

"We can get this poverty lark down to a fine art!" I said cheerfully.

"Do you have to be so insensitive? We probably won't be poor forever! Not like real poor people! You're almost bragging about it! Anyone would think you were making a lifestyle choice! Yuck!"

"I'm just trying to make it a bit more amusing!"

"Well, it isn't amusing. But I will have a look at the skip with you. I like skips."

The skip was outside a petrol station and they seemed to be changing their displays. There was the most beautiful metal rack designed to hold chewing gum. I fell in love with it immediately.

"Look - double mint, juicy fruit, how fabulous is that?"

"It's lovely, but. We'll have to carry it."

"I know! It's not far."

"To school! My school!"

"I'll blame it on you - say - tut! - you know what teenagers are like! Their bedrooms!"

"Sometimes I think you're the teenager," Nancy said, with just a touch of - what was it? resignation? Despair? Horror?

Chapter 3

Trouting with Trumpeter's Lips

My very first date was with a chap called Rory. I really liked his name. (How sad. As Nancy pointed out to me.)

"I think with a name like Rory he must be fairly interesting. I mean, if he was called, say, David, that could mean anything. There could be infinite varieties of Davids. But a Rory has to be -"

"Mother!" Nancy interrupted.

"What?"

"I can't believe how naïve you're being about this. Are you meeting him in a public place?"

"Yes. But it's a really nice name."

"It really is a creepy name. Don't give him your address, and don't tell him too much about yourself. He could be anyone! What if he really wants to meet young girls? Have you told him about me?"

"No! As if! I may be mad, but I'm not stupid!" The family motto.

"And what do you know about him? What does he do? How old

is he?"

"He's fifty -"

"Ugh - old and wrinkly!"

"Nice and mature, grown up children, ooh, and get this, his wife ran away with his son's best friend. He's a musician."

"Humph," said Nancy, going back to her revision. "Sad. I bet."

I prepared for the date by getting rid of a lot of hair from different parts of my body, which took ages. I read later in a magazine that this is unnecessary unless one expects to sleep with the man on the first date, but I was still learning at this stage. Then I brushed my teeth three times and put lots of make-up on. Then I got dressed and got make-up all over the front of my dress when I put it over my head.

"Oh, no! Look what I did! How could I be so stupid!"

Nancy heard my cries and came and sat patiently on the bed while I tried on a series of alternative outfits. Eventually we agreed that the jeans and sparkly top with a jacket would do.

"Can I get on with my work now?"

"Earrings? Necklace - what? Brooch? Tell me and then you can go."

Finally I was dressed and had on my rather nice ankle boots too. Still half an hour to go. I put Led Zeppelin on very loud and danced around to calm my nerves.

"Mum!"

It was Nancy in the doorway. "What?"

"I can't concentrate! Couldn't you hear me yelling for you to turn it down?"

"Well I'm nervous."

"Can't you have a drink or something like normal mad mothers?"

"Drink - that's a good idea," I said, forgetting the night I had been out with Carla. I rummaged about in the drinks cupboard (they won't let you have alcohol when your furniture is in storage so our collection of world liqueurs was taking up valuable storage space in the tiny flat.)

"Oooh there's all sorts in here," I squeaked excitedly a few moments later. What's this? Laphroaig?! Yummy! I'll have some of that."

I poured myself a mighty slug and drank it. Nancy was right, I did feel calmer. I felt relaxed and cheerful.

"Alright I'm off now," I called as I departed. "I'll have been last seen in the Queen's Arms if you have to inform the police. And you know what I was wearing."

"I hope the Queen is fit!" was her parting shot.

I teetered down the road in my ankle boots feeling rather sexy and fabulous. The Queen's Arms was not far away and I had been in there a few times before, as a married woman. Now here I was, a dangerous divorcee on the prowl in the jeans that hadn't fitted her for ages. Unbidden thoughts scuttered round my head like rats in the attic. What if Rory was really gorgeous and attractive? What if we fell in love at first sight, got married and did up an old farmhouse and went to live in the South of France? What if I wrote the lyrics and he wrote the music and we wrote an opera together? What kind of musician was he again?

I tottered into the Queen's Arms, mentally making Nancy's joke again, and peered into the public bar. It was deserted apart from a very old man wheezily moaning to a fat woman in green. I closed the door again and opened the lounge bar door. The lounge bar was deserted and smelled unpleasantly of air freshener. I went self-consciously in and ordered a glass of wine. The barman was very polite indeed, and it occurred to me that I could have had this kind of service all my life if only I had put more make-up on. Gertrude definitely had the right idea, painting an inch thick, if you ask me. Which Nancy never does. I wondered what kind of makeup Gertrude had access to - white lead and pig's blood, I vaguely remembered reading once.

While I was waiting and thinking about Elizabethan cosmetics I gazed about me and noted the fine collection of brass, the real fire and the footrest at the bar with approval. I was less impressed by the stained velour upholstery and the badger's head over the ladies' toilets.

I sat there for a while. It was very quiet. Suddenly, a man came in. He looked at me and then went out again. He was in and out so fast that I failed to form an impression of him. I sipped my wine anxiously. The man came back. I was sure he was the same one.

"Is it Holly?"

"Yes," I said, standing up.

"Rory," he said. We shook hands, and had a good look at each other. He was a very outdoorsy type of dresser, very khaki, those trousers with lots of pockets, trainer sort of shoes, very rustly jacket which he removed deafeningly. A rambling man. When it went quiet again we sat down and he rolled up his sleeves (quite a nice stripy jumper), grinning at me as if he was getting to work. He had that kind of facial hair which hasn't made up its mind if it's a beard yet.

"You're not quite what I expected from your ad," he said.

"No?" I was a bit alarmed by this opening gambit. How was I supposed to reply?

"No. You're a bit of a tart, aren't you?"

"What? Am I? Gosh. I didn't think so."

"I quite like tarts," he added, in what he seemed to think was a placatory manner.

I had already decided that I would never meet Rory ever again if I could help it, but also simultaneously decided to stay a bit longer, to find out what other outrageous things he might say to me. I was intrigued.

"Have you been out with many tarts?" I asked

"Oh, most women are tarts," he said, "but you didn't sound like one. In your advert. So I was a bit surprised."

"I see."

"But now I see you, you're very much the usual kind of tart."

"Which is what?"

"Oh," he said vaguely, waving his hands in circular movements in the air (whatever that means), "you know, high heels and all that muck on your face."

"It's called fashion. And stuff. You know."

"Oh, I know that. But you don't have to be a slave to it, do you? I mean, take someone like Kate Winslet. Simple, natural beauty speaks for itself."

"Hmmm. But you can't find a simple natural beauty like Kate Winslet?"

"No," he said, gloomily.

"Maybe you're not looking in the right places. Have you tried Hollywood?"

"I mean," he added, a little late, "you look very nice and all that. Nice hair. Do you want to go for a walk at the weekend? I know some very nice caves we could explore together. I can lend you a hard hat. Would you like that?"

Later, I was to learn that there are a lot of Rories. Just at that moment I thought I was uniquely cursed with having to be on a date with the weirdest man in the world. What a lot I had to learn, readers! Actually Rory was quite nice, I now realise, looking back. In comparison. In chapter four, I will give you a thoughtfully produced, never-before-so-comprehensively surveyed list of the kind of men you can expect to encounter if you are brave enough to attempt to find a partner when you're over forty. But you'll have to wait for that, or you'll miss some good bits in this chapter.

Back at work I told Carla about Rory. She laughed a lot, so much that she made herself cough. She had given up the cigars and was back on the Silk Cut.

"Poor man," she said, when she got her breath back, "I wonder if he will ever find the girl of his dreams? It seems impossible - and yet - it happens. What sort of musician did you say he was?"

"A music teacher in a comprehensive."

"Aha. Maybe one of his pupils will be the piece of cake."

"At least I didn't get drunk, I wasn't there long enough. The weird thing is he keeps leaving messages on my phone saying he thought it went really well, and can he see me again."

"Oh this is normal, my darling. Men are so obtuse."

"So have you got a boyfriend at the moment, Carla?"

"No," she said in a way that did not encourage further questioning. But true to my inability to get subliminal messages, I ploughed on.

"Why is that, then?"

"My last boyfriend," she said, staring at me in a hostile manner that made me feel uncomfortable, "threatened to kill me. He stalked me. It for some reason put me off men for a while. Any more questions?"

"I'm sorry," I said. "Where is he now?"

"I don't know. Last I heard, he went to Spain. I hope never to see him again."

"Is he from round here?"

"He is English, I don't know where he is from, exactly, he was always a bit quiet when I talked about his family. I met him here, in Milltown. We lived together for two months, but it went crazy and I threw him out, which was when he threatened me."

"What does he look like?" I was thinking of the man in the pub.

"Tall, red hair, very piercing blue eyes I thought were so very very English. Ha!"

"How scary," I said. "But easy to spot."

"Yes. Scary. It put me off Englishmen for a while."

"Yes. Mind you, there are nutters in every country I expect."

"Nutters, that is a good word. Ah well, our ten minutes is up, back to the headsets." Where, speaking of nutters, I seemed to be talking to most of the French ones.

"Where are you in England? I come over to England, I could meet you and take you to lunch..."

"Ah, oui, you can ask me more questions of course. I am happy with my computer. I don't need any more computers, thank you. But I would like to talk to you, tell me, what you are wearing...?" Or:

"You have blonde hair, yes, and - "

"No," I interrupted crossly, "I do not. I have dark brown hair - with, um, reddish highlights - and hazel eyes. I am not a little English girl. I am a grown woman."

"The English women - they are so frank -"
"Holly!"
It was Martine.
"Yes, Martine?"
"Will you please stay in the script?"
"Well, I would love to, if only other people would do the same. They just won't be professional. I am trying so hard to talk about monitors, Martine. They will insist on flirting all the time."
"It is up to you to keep them in the script. That is your job," she added menacingly, with the emphasis on the word job.
"I will try harder, I promise."
But no matter how hard I tried, my English accent was so alluring to the French businessmen (presumably bored to death in grey French offices while the French spring the real deal - was happening all around them) that they couldn't help wandering down the primrose paths of flirtation. Monitors were nothing to them, compared to the opportunity to have a jolly chat with a little English girl. I was a free international sex line. I knew where it would lead, and it did. One day Martine intercepted me at home time, and told me I wasn't needed any more.
"Oh, no," I said.
I went back to the jobcentre. They told me that I was now an experienced call centre worker and officially computer literate (yes! Result!) and so they could put me forward for other jobs in the area, but it would not pay so well because it was not in French. So began my career ringing people all over the country and pestering them to take an interest in things of which they had previously, in most cases, not even heard. Milltown, fortunately for me, was a mecca for people who wanted to set up call centres, as the Yorkshire accent was thought to be friendly and persuasive. The fact that my accent was not terribly Yorkshire any more after years of international travel and sophisticated living with Mr Meansod, an unreconstructed southerner, was, fortunately, not too much of an issue. Also Milltown contained many mills, ripe for conversion to call centres. Instead of the deafening clatter of looms, there arose

the chatter of a thousand persuasive northerners.

All my contracts were short-term, as I didn't really fit the classic twenty-something profile, but the young people who were my jolly co-workers adopted me cheerfully enough and even offered to take me out to show me the club scene in the city. Nancy found this hilarious.

"You can't go out clubbing at your age, mother! Only old slappers in leopard print leggings go clubbing!"

"I thought leggings were back? And what about stereotyping! What if I said all teenagers loaf about all day and take drugs all night?"

"I do know a few like that."

"Well then stop knowing them immediately. Is it that Jack?"

"God, mother, you really have got an imagination, haven't you? What do you think of me? I'm not taking drugs, ok? It would interfere with my brain function, eddit? Brain? needed for exams? Grow up."

"So you do intend to pass your exams? That's good news."

"Well, how else am I going to get out of here?"

"Oh that's nice! You could get a job near here and live with me and help to run the house! Think how lovely that would be. Just the two of us girls forever."

"Ma dear, I'm going to go to university and have a career - if I've learnt nothing else from you, it's that a woman needs to have control of her own life and not leave it to a man to sort her out."

"I do not need a man to sort me out!" I said indignantly.

"I know you don't. That's the whole point. No woman does."

"But it would be nice to have a snog - or a bit of -"

"For goodness sake, too much information!"

"Alright, let's not talk about this any more. I'll be good if you'll be good. Let's be honest with each other, but not too much detail, ok?"

"Fine. Now let me get on with my revision."

Which was Nancy's constant refrain, making it difficult to have long conversations. I suspected she was avoiding talking to me, but it was impossible for me to work out what was going on in her head. She loved her dad, of course, and was presumably feeling very confused. I couldn't make it all better, no matter how hard I tried. We were just going to have to play it by ear - life had suddenly become a vicious game where other people made all the rules but wouldn't tell you what they were; they only yelled at you if you broke them. Hockey had always been like that to me. My God. Life had become a compulsory triple period of hockey, all the time. What a terrible fate.

"So can I go clubbing, or what?"

Nancy took off her glasses and put them wearily on the table. She looked up from her book, and sighed. Suddenly she looked like my grandpa.

"I suppose so. As long as you don't get back late, making a row, because I need my sleep. And as long as you don't go to the same clubs that me and my friends go to," she added firmly.

"Now please. Can I have a bit of peace and quiet?"

So that you can listen to the evening news on the wireless set, I suppose, I thought. But not wishing to antagonise the poor child (after all she had enough to put up with) I contented myself with tiptoeing out of the room in an exaggerated manner. Three days later I found myself boogieing on down in Swizzle, a club where most of the women seemed to be too thin to be actual women. It was in Leeds, one of our local cities (how lucky we are to have more than one).

"Are you sure this isn't a transvestite place?" I nervously asked Jimmy, one of the lovely young people who had dragged Granny along to show her a good time.

"There could be all sorts here," he bellowed over the deafening boom of the bass. "Who cares anyway?"

I began to get into my dancing stride and remembered a few seventies moves which made people around me edge away a bit. Gave me a bit of room to express myself. I reached that point when one is practically in a trance and was just thinking that I must do more of this, when I was interrupted by a tap on my shoulder. I (literally) spun round to see a short, spotty sixteen year old smiling in what he clearly imagined to be an engaging way.

"Hi." he said, or rather shouted, "I was watching you. Can I dance with you?"

"Er." I said. I didn't like to be rude. "Hi. Go on then."

We started dancing. He was actually quite good at dancing.

"How old are you?" I yelled.

"Twenty-two," he shouted back. "I have ID. Here -" he started to feel in his pockets.

"It's alright," I shouted, "I believe you."

We danced for a bit. Suddenly seeming to tire of all the idle chit-chat he moved closer and slipped a sweaty hand round my waist.

"Oi!" I shrieked, "stop that!"

"But why?" his mouth was right next to my ear. "You like it, don't you."

"No I don't! You're a child!"

Looking around in a bit of a panic I saw, not far away, Jimmy dancing with Naz, one of the girls who had been working with me on a particularly unexciting mobile phone promotion. I was dancing alongside them in a flash. The spotty youth followed and danced in orbit around us, looking expectant.

"Fuck off and stop harassing my mother," Jimmy told him, having sized up the situation with admirable speed. The youth melted into the field, a horrified look on his face.

"Oh thank you," I said fervently to Jimmy. "I'll be more careful in future."

I danced after that as if I were a member of a religious sect who danced for purely holy purposes. I ignored any taps on my shoulder and adopted (after studying my fellow terpsichorean zealots) the glazed facial expression of someone whacked out on illegal uppers, or it might be downers.

Jimmy, Naz and the other call centre drones (they were actually quite possible to tell apart after a while) swept me up in time to get to the last train home.

"We need to get you home before you get off with any more underage totty," they sniggered.

"I was just trying to be nice to him."

"You'll be done for kiddy fiddling if you're not careful." More laughter.

"You mustn't be nice to men," said Jen, a normally silent blonde. We were sitting in the station bar, waiting for the trains to Milltown and Morton Spa. Their train was a bit earlier than mine. "They just think you're soft, and that they can take advantage of you. Better that they're a bit scared of you."

"Really?"

"Oh yes," Naz agreed.

"Even I think so," said Jimmy. "You mustn't give off victim vibes, or they'll tear you to pieces."

"Oh heck. This is reminding me of feminist meetings in the seventies."

"We're all feminists now," Jimmy said. "Even some Yorkshiremen."

"Even you?"

"Especially me."

"But I don't want men to be scared of me."

"It's for your own protection. It's a bad world out there, Holly."

"I've always found it charming, up till now. I've had a lovely life, most of the time. I used to have an Aga, and a Smallbone of Devizes kitchen. I used to go to the opera, regularly. And to the Maldives at Christmas. I don't mind being poor, I've been poor before, when I was first married. It's a challenge. You don't just run away from it, do you?"

I was just a tiny bit drunk, but the lovely young people had to leave me, to get their train. I was alone at the table, just managing not to mutter aloud to myself about planting climbing roses and keeping bees. I had been alone for approximately two minutes when a man weaved, or wove, across to my table. He was very drunk. I was virginally sober compared to him.

"Ullo," he said, "you have a nice face. You look like you understand."

"Oh? Do I? How misleading."

"My wife is going to kill me when I get in."

"Why? What have you done?"

"I bought a boat," he said. Tears welled in his eyes. "It's a beauty. But she won't understand. I want to sail it across the Atlantic. And then round the world. But she'll just think I'm off me head."

"That's - possible."

"What will I say to her? How will I explain? How do I get her to have sex with me ever again after this?"

I wondered briefly how much I ought to charge for this clearly specialised service, but decided in the end not to charge at all. Spread the love.

"Tell her you've bought it for her. As a present. And that you've named it the - what's her name?"

"Marie."

"Perfect - Maria, Star of the Sea. Stella Maris."

"What?"

"Just say you called it after her."

"Will you write that down for me?"

I wrote it on his cigarette packet, and passed it back to him. His red rimmed eyes gazed into mine.

"And will you sleep with me if she won't?"

"Absolutely not."

"Oh." He looked a bit upset. "Well, I have to get me train."

"Good luck!"

I was alone at my table again. For thirty whole seconds.

"You look like a nice lady." He was a new one. Very drunk indeed. Even worse than the last one. Thirtyish, balding, stocky, a horny-handed son of toil.

"Do I. Hmm."

I should have a sign saying The Doctor Is In, I thought.

"It's teeming with rain out there. It's the sky cryin' like me."

"I see."

"Cryin' for my life. It's all been a waste. You know wha' it's like - going home -"

"I should think it's very nice, warm and cosy with lovely people waiting for you."

"Naw. It ain't like that at all."

There was a pause. I wondered if I was expected to say something. I cleared my throat.

"Well that's a pity." James Blunt came on the piped music system. Somehow it seemed appropriate.

"I could fall in love wi' you," he said suddenly.

"Well," I said firmly, "unfortunately I have a train to catch and you'll never see me again, otherwise, who knows what might have happened?"

So saying I escaped from the bar with my handbag strap diagonally across my body in the approved anti-mugging style, feeling pleased that I was clearly able to look after myself as far as odd men were concerned. If I had acquired no other useful skills lately, I had at least learnt to detect a nutter and fend him off.

I got home just as Nancy was disappearing into her room with a mug of cocoa. Her bright hair fell down onto her Little Miss Naughty dressing gown.

"Good night, my darling," I said, falling on her neck to sniff it as was my wont.

"Yes, alright," she said impatiently disentangling herself, "I need my sleep you know. I hope you're not going to have the radio on."

"Only the shipping forecast," I said meekly.

Chapter 4

Thick Repeaters

So - I promised you a comprehensive list. Here it is.

The man who is really looking for Kate Winslet/Julia Roberts/Dawn French/Imelda Marcos whatever. This man is not properly grown up. He may have endearing qualities, but attempts to get you to look or behave or sound more like Kate, Julia, Imelda or Dawn will lead only to frustration on both sides. He needs to learn to like real people. It's a bit like when you were a teenager and had a crush on David Cassidy or Marc Bolan or heaven forbid - George Michael. Run away from this one. You will never be the real thing.

The man who is after your money. We have all read about him in the papers. Not as easy to spot as you might assume. He may well appear to be perfect in every way. Please remember that apparent perfection is suspicious in itself. The bit of rough. He is probably also younger than you. After a while, your constant references to Mozart operas and ability to name plants in Latin will get on his nerves, if not drive him completely crazy. In the short term, though, he is great to have around if you are doing up a house, as he is very handy with a drill.

The man who wants a baby. If you want a baby, this could be the man for you. But, please bear in mind, if you are over forty, your eggs will be a bit dodgy by now, if not actually curdled. After a few unsuccessful tries, it may turn out that it's not actually you he loves so much, but the idea of reproduction. Lots of little copies of him. I think he may be a bit of an egotist. If you don't want a baby, run away, no matter how rich, sexy or charming he may be.

The man who thinks he is better looking than you. Especially if he also works out every day and thinks he is very fit. Run, but make sure you get a head start with this one, as he is probably quite fast. You may have to create a diversion.

The man who expresses an interest in swinging or threesomes. No matter how casually this is dropped into the conversation on date three, this is his real interest. You may also be interested in this, in which case, pick up the hint and go for it. Otherwise, run like the wind.

The man who has just got divorced because his wife has had an affair. He is not feeling too charitable towards women generally, in fact, like Malvolio at the end of Twelfth Night, he intends to "be revenged on the whole pack of them", starting with you. He will probably be very nice to start with and then suddenly dump you without explanation. Be prepared.

The very jolly looking man; an interesting specimen, he is usually terminally gloomy about everything and will contradict everything you say. He will also complain all the time about how miserable other people are. The contradiction between his appearance and his conversation will drive you mad after only a very short conversation. Never give this type your phone number, as he will never realise he has been dumped and will keep ringing you to complain about the world.

The man who smokes too much weed/ does too much coke/ drinks too much anything. Not always obvious at first. Does he sniff a lot? Check his bins, especially the glass bin. Easy to run away from. He will probably not even notice for a while that you have gone.

By way of contrast: the reformed alcoholic. Like going out with a priest. You may be into that kind of thing, in which case I am told AA meetings are ideal pick-up joints. The professional gambler. Particularly if you have any money, or a house. Or a car. Or even a couple of pairs of nice earrings.

The man who says he is in love with you on the second date. He is desperate. He may also fall into one or more of the other categories, but this attribute alone should put you on your guard.

The married man. Obvious, but need to be mentioned; after all, this is a COMPREHENSIVE list. My favourite version is the one who tells you that he is married, but his wife hasn't had sex with him for twenty years because she has a medical problem. Clearly he thinks you are a free whore. All the usual caveats apply.

The really appalling dresser. He has not been paying attention to ANYTHING.

The much older man. You may feel that this is a mainly platonic deal, and that you are not expected to fetch him his cocoa with his late-night viagra. You would be wrong. Sooner or later he will pounce, saying stuff like he is only flesh and blood after all (as if! As Nancy would say. He is made of mothballs). Run away, before you are overpowered by the smell of dust.

The much younger man. This seems, at first, to be an attractive option. Bear in mind, though, that he is not used to cellulite and will wonder what has happened to your thighs to make them like that. He might even ask, worrying that you have some disease or have been in a terrible accident with boiling water. You may feel obliged to regurgitate MarieClaire's views on the subject of the causes of cellulite (the magazine, do keep up). You could end up sitting up half the night talking about cellulite, which is not very sexy. Yes, alright, this happened to me.

The man who suspects you are a man in drag. No need to say any more about him.

The man who is still in love with his teenage beloved. Oh dear. He is doomed.

The dancing man. This is a weird one. I always thought men who danced were a good thing, sort of dancing/having a sense of rhythm equals sexy equation, but it turns out that men who do samba, jazz dancing, ceroc, jive or similar related dance routines are all sexcrazed weirdos. I suspect they go to the classes with the sole intention of laying hands on a variety of women in a legitimate context, while showing off how well they twirl. This is based, as are all my categories, on empirical evidence. However I am willing to accept that there are men who do the above mentioned dancing who are not weirdos, all I know is, I haven't met any of them.

The man who is in therapy. Unless this is purely to address the issues which have arisen from a divorce or bereavement (which would be a good thing), he may be in a permanent state of loopiness. Run very fast if he says his therapist reckons he has OCD, ADD, or any kind of Attachment Disorder.

The soppy man. This one has usually been married already. He likes pet names and "snuggling". You may like this too, in which case, he is the one for you. You will be given cuddly toys on Valentine's day.

The man who goes on about the dangerousness of his ex-girlfriend. Apparently she stalked him, read his text messages and knew his pin number. He thinks most woman are like this. He thinks (no, he knows) that you are like this. He really doesn't like women, does he?

The man who still lives at home with his mother. Even if this is post divorce, I would steer well clear.

The man who thinks you should cover up a bit.

The man who lives in an excessively tidy and minimalist house. (Unless you like that kind of thing yourself. But bear in mind he will expect you to be in charge of keeping it that way.)

There you go. That's my list. Feel free to add to it. I'll leave a space.

Chapter 5

Opening the Hangar Doors

You'll have got the idea, from the preceding chapter, that I had a lot of weird dates over the next month, and you'd be right. My advert brought in one hundred and eight replies, so it was lucky I was working and could afford the phone bill again. Every night I listened to the distant, recorded thoughts of men I had never met, and made short notes. (Sounds lovely! Sounds nice. Sounds alright. Sounds odd. Sounds creepy. Ugh.)

And this is how I met the man of my dreams.

There was a lot of speculation, among my prospective suitors (as Nancy insisted on calling them) as to the exact nature of sexy shoes. Did I mean Gucci, or what, they demanded petulantly. One enquired whether diamante pit boots would fit the bill. I never actually got to meet him, probably I should have. They turned up in all sorts of footwear which they fondly imagined to be sexy, from sandals to crocodile loafers. It was a major insight into the male psyche, I could have written a paper on it afterwards of enormous anthropological significance. If only I had had time.

During this fruitful and thoughtful time ("you have a wonderful voice. You sound like a woman, not a recipe. Your message is so seductive. Friendship is people reflecting each other's solitude. You sound like a sex goddess. You sound like Nigella Lawson"), Basil rang me to inform me that there were still some "blockages in the pipeline" which was code for no deal. But, he added, that was no reason why I shouldn't buy a house, because I was bound to get the money eventually. So as well as working full time, I now began to look for the perfect house for Nancy and me.

"All these house are horrible!" Nancy exclaimed, throwing aside all the brochures I had collected at great length from every possible local estate agent. "I don't want to live in any of them. Why can't we stay here?"

"But part of the point is that I need to invest, darling, in property. I don't have any other investments."

"Well buy a house in France or something, then," said Nancy, igniting in me a blue touch paper which subsequently exploded.

Very late one night, I was surfing the internet (I had bought a computer, hoorah!) and I had had a couple of glasses of wine. Oh all right then, two thirds of a bottle. (Which is a couple of glasses in some bars.) I was just finishing it off, for the glass bin. (Tidy, you see.) I found a super TV programme about buying a house abroad, it had a wonderful website with tips about where to buy and so on. As I read on, tipsily, I read the bit about "if you would like to take part in the show, please email ... ", my mouse clicked without prompting, and soon I was composing an email to Goodfun productions about how I wanted to buy a house in France.

The next morning, probably owing to the early onset of alcohol-related dementia, I had no recollection of this whatsoever.

At work we were doing another promotion of computer monitors. In English, this time. Thank God. I had a list of English people to work through.

"We have a special promotion on at the moment on computer monitors," I recited into my microphone, reading off the screen.

"What is a computer monitor?" asked the well-educated sounding voice at the other end. I looked at my contact list again. Who was this idiot? It was the office of the Sergeant at Arms, the House of Commons.

"Er - it's the bit you look at," I said, helplessly. "The, er, telly thing, I think. Like a telly. But it's a computer screen."

"I have no idea what you're talking about," said Well-Educated Voice, ringing off.

At lunchtime, I met up with Carla, because for this short time we were working in the same building again.

"How is your love life?" she asked, scowling.

"I can look after myself you know."

"I don't think so. Have you met anyone special?"

"I think I might have."

This was true. I had a met a particularly excitable sailor, and as I had always wanted to learn to sail ever since I had read Swallows and Amazons as a small girl, I was rather keen. The fact that he wanted a baby (see preceding chapter) was not particularly bothering me as we had spectacular chemical attraction and I was scheming to get Nancy out of the way so I could commit adultery (my divorce not yet through). He had turned up for the first date in particularly hideous and unsexy shoes (slip-ons) but this faux-pas had not prevented me from going literally weak at the knees when he kissed me. It was like being seventeen all over again. Yes! Bring on the sex part!

"Tell me about him," Carla demanded.

"Well, I don't know him very well yet, but he's promising."

"Blond or brun?"

"Isn't that tobacco? You are obsessed. Blond."

"This makes sense, as you are dark. Has he got money?"

"I don't think so, he lives in a tiny little house."

"I think you need money."

"I don't. I'm a self-sufficient woman."

Carla snorted a bit at this, which I felt was about her rather than me, so I remained aloof.

"I think you have expensive tastes. Holly, you will learn," she said, laughing in what I felt to be an unnecessarily patronising way.

"And how is your love life, Carla?"

"Oh, you know, not enough sex. Too much wanting shirts ironing. Same old same old," she said, gloomily.

"It's good that lots of men still want to go out with you, though, isn't it?" I said, trying to sound encouraging.

"I suppose you think I should settle down before it's too late," she said crossly. "So many people say to me the same thing. Oh, Carla, you should decide soon because your sell-by date is approaching. This sell-by date! What does this mean? What an insult!"

"I didn't mean that at all. I just meant that you are so attractive to men. That's a good thing, isn't it?" I didn't add, at forty-nine.

"I suppose so. I am just fed up, Holly, we must go out for a drink again. I need to be with my women friends again. So soothing."

We made a date, and Carla drifted back to schmoozing Italian businessmen, while I attempted to talk to British senior managers about computers. I had devised a strategy for getting past secretaries. It was complicated because they were there at least partly to filter out people like me. I was a pest, an intrusion: the fly in the business ointment. For example: the list said Nicholas Jenkins, IT Director.

"Hello, I need to speak to Nick," I said in my best RP, not a trace of comforting Yorkshire to be heard.

"Oh," said a flustered female voice. "He's in a meeting."

"He'll speak to me," I boomed.

"Nick Jenkins."

"Hello, I'm ringing you about computer monitors.."

"How did you get this number? Sally! Why has this woman been put through?"

Because she thinks I'm your wife or possibly your mistress, and she doesn't want to upset you, I sniggered to myself, mentally chalking up Holly Field 1, masters of the universe 0. The only way, it seemed to me, to do the job was to think of it as an elaborate game, with rules that were made up as we went along. I couldn't allow myself to think how irritating I was, my contract was to get through to the contact, mission impossible style. As I telephonically parachuted into the war zone of high powered business, I congratulated myself on my skill and ingenuity. There was an adrenaline rush. So, it wasn't really fun, but I was good at pretending. How like marriage.

Nancy, meanwhile, had embarked on the elaborate game which is the public examination system. It was similar. However, whereas I came home exhilarated by my jousts with corporate blockage, Nancy came home exhausted and extremely grumpy. I had stopped having normal conversations with her, it was just:

"Was it Physics?"

"Hate Physics."

(Pause).

"Beans on toast?"

"Hate beans."

You don't usually. You always like beans. Don't say it. Keep it light. Fluffy. Don't mention the war.

"Bacon buttie? Darling?" (Voice unnaturally high, have to clear throat.)

"Go on then."

"Red or brown?"

"Brown."

"White or brown? Sweetie?"

"Oh God, do I have to decide? Well, if I have a choice, which I doubt, white. Then."

"Actually. You do have a choice, I have a white loaf in the freezer."

"Cool."

Well, yes, extremely cool. Frozen actually. Solid. More blue than white, really. But what are miFieldaves for? She was very annoying. But I remembered my own exam experiences, sympathised and braced myself for more horror.

"Darling? Do you need the computer?"

Nancy did not reply but simply waved her biology text book under my nose. I fell silent, and crept off to the kitchen, while Nancy covered the dining table with bits of paper weighted with glasses of water and fat books.

Chapter 5. Opening the Hangar Doors

Over tea I asked her (tactfully) again if she needed the computer. "You're not looking for men on it, are you?" she asked sternly.

"No, just want to see if I have any emails."

"Good. Go on then. Be my guest. "

"Thank you, darling."

There was one from him! The sexy sailor. Hoorah, I had a date for Saturday. I was so excited by this that I almost shut down the computer without opening my other new email. It was from Goodfun Productions. They wanted Nancy and me to be on the show. Their researcher would ring me to find out what I was looking for. Omigod. I decided I wouldn't tell Nancy just yet, as she would almost certainly hit the roof. I printed off the email from Roger, the sailor, as I wanted to read it over and over again in the privacy of my bedroom.

"hi Holly," it began ordinarily enough, "I just wanted to tell you that I have been thinking about you constantly since I met you." Constantly! "I can't forget that dress you were wearing, and find myself thinking about what is underneath... Can I take you to dinner on Saturday? I am free all day, so perhaps we could go for a walk in the afternoon. I really want to get to know you."

I was so thrilled by this romantic poppycock (I didn't think it WAS poppycock, dearest readers) that I started planning to have sex on Saturday, and to do this I needed to get Nancy out of the way, as she would never stand for it. (It was a bit like being a teenager with intolerant parents, all over again).

"Nancy," I began.

She took off her glasses in the accustomed mock-patient way and frowned at me.

"What?"

"Would you like to stay with one of your friends on Saturday night? Jess maybe? You could have a bit of a break from your studying, get out on the town for an evening, let your hair down..."

I trailed off as Nancy's expression had become more scowly and suspicious than ever.

"Why?"

"Well, because it would be nice for you and, er,"
"And?"
"And I have a date."
"So?"
"So, I don't think you're ready to meet any of my, er,"
"Suitors?"
"Gosh what an old fashioned word," I laughed nervously.
"Shags?"
"Honestly Nancy."
"Alright I'll go to Jess's on Saturday," she said, putting the glasses back on, "it'll be nice to get a bit of peace for a change. We can do some revision together, she's really good at chemistry."

"Tell me about your daughter," said Roger as we set off to climb the side of the moor (did I mention Morton Spa was on the side of a moor?) on Saturday afternoon. He was into children, I reminded myself, because his mind was on reproduction. So was mine, for that matter, but I was planning to just go through the motions, as it were, without letting any actual gametes have contact with one another.

"She's sixteen, doing her GCSEs. She wants to be a doctor. She's a dear girl but a bit stressed at the moment. It'll be better for you to meet her later. When it's all over. The ghastly exams," I clarified babblingly.

"I nearly did medicine," he said, "But at the last minute I decided to switch to chemistry. I'm glad I did, because now I have this job I love."

"Wow, you must meet Nancy - er - eventually," I said, "she'll have a lot in common with you. I didn't realise you were a scientist."

"Well obviously I'm not now," he laughed apologetically, "just a capitalist these days."

"There's nothing wrong with that," I said, cautiously, my mind re-examining the evidence I had seen of Roger's financial situation. Perhaps he was better off than I had been assuming? Not that it mattered, obviously... apart from the fact that a rich boyfriend would reacquaint me with all my decadent pre-redundancy married habits. Oooh, but did I want to go back to all that? Particularly if it in any way involved small people being sick on me?

Here you are again, I told myself irritably, speculating about a future with a man you've only just met. Just stop it now. He might be a con man and rapist, and here you are wandering off on a lonely moor with him, and who knows where you are?

Actually this was all ok really as I had casually told him I had left a note for Nancy just before I set off, with all the details of where I was going and, more importantly, who I was with and what time I would be back. It was like being eight again. Dear mum I'm going to deborahs to wotch batman I can have tea with her alright love from Holly

So at least if I was murdered they would have a lot of clues, assuming he didn't steal my keys and go and destroy all the evidence and wait for Nancy and murder her too. But he didn't know where I lived, so that was alright, at least not yet, but he soon would if I carried through my seduction attempt.

All this complication was running through my head while Roger was telling me the details of what he did for a living so I missed most of the finer points, but gathered that he was some sort of biggish cheese in some sort of business that made something or other.

"Oh - do you have a factory? I love factories," I exclaimed truthfully, "I used to draw them all the time when I was little."

"Yes, there is a factory. I'm sure you'll be allowed to draw it if you want to."

He looked at me a bit oddly. I felt that my powers of reading what other people meant by their expressions was definitely improving, and that this one meant, "you're completely mad, but in a nice way." I think he was also assessing me for motherhood potential but I didn't like to think about this so dismissed it from my mind, to allow more lustful thoughts to flood in instead.

I considered Roger's physical attributes (what I could make out under the waterproof layers - it was yet another of those days when at least we shouldn't grumble as we should be grateful not to be having forest fires like those Australians.) He appeared to have nice broad shoulders for heaving on ropes and whatnot, big hands for gripping ditto (and gripping other things I thought a little deliriously), tousled but attractive hair and a generally weatherbeaten complexion. Yummy.

"So what kind of factory is it then?"

"We make paint. It's a paint factory."

"Is it at all eco friendly?" I asked cautiously, not wanting to frighten him off if he didn't give a fig about the environment, since I was still planning to lure him into bed in any case (I would just have to dump him straight away afterwards or Nancy would kill me) so I was highly relieved when he said it was special organic paint and that they recycled things and had cycle to work schemes and a healthy eating canteen and worried a great deal about environmental issues. Phew.

"Roger," I said, panting a bit because he was heading uphill at a hell of a lick and I was trying to keep up, "why aren't you married?"

"Oh," he said casually, not even stopping to look me in the eye (with his piercing Old Salt blue eyes), "I'm what they used to call manic depressive, now they call it bipolar, I've had a bit of trouble with relationships. But I'm on a new medication, it's made quite a difference. And I've decided that having a family would settle me down. "

I was literally stopped in my tracks by this and it was a while before Roger noticed that I was no longer panting just a few feet behind his right shoulder, but was stranded by an exhausted looking gorse bush unable to think of one sensible remark.

"You see," I said, probably tactlessly, as he descended to rejoin me, "I was thinking that you seemed such a jolly good catch but I suppose this explains a lot. Gosh."

"Yes, it does explain a lot, as you put it."

"Well I'm cool with it," I said cheerfully. "I mean, we all have our mad moments don't we, I know I do."

"Good. I mean, good that you're cool, not good that you have mad moments."

"Isn't that a bit unreasonable -" I was beginning when I realised he was laughing at me, in a nice way, something which often for some reason turns me on, and I had a massive surge of fancying him which propelled me uphill and into his arms where we had a massive hillside snog. We only stopped when some elderly dog walkers went past audibly snorting indignantly, though the dog audibly sniffed us with great interest. Plainly the dog, unlike his owners, understood about LOVE.

Because, dear reader, that was what I was falling in - I really felt dizzy and as if I was about to fall over - I was getting rather weak and feeble with LOVE. Really really I was. I hadn't felt like this for so long that at first I thought I must be coming down with something nasty - there had been a bit of a bug going round the call centre, which was an overheated tightly sealed double glazed petri dish of a building. But actually I was suffering from the oldest heart condition in the world and firmly closing my eyes to all Roger's bad points - what bad points? He was the most amazing, perfect man I had ever met!

We had a magical walk, most of the details of which entirely eluded me because I was wallowing in fantasies about my future with lovely Roger, sailing the Mediterranean all summer and the Caribbean all winter, having lots of lovely sex and drinking lots of lovely wine, and making sure at all times that we had copious supplies of Roger's medication. And contraception.

I know we saw a stone circle, because Roger told me all about the points of the compass and navigating by the sun and I nearly got the giggles when he said sextant but managed to control myself. We also saw flowers blooming, buds opening, birds singing and the sun actually came out for a short while, but then went hastily back in again as if it had wandered out on a whim and suddenly realised that its wife would be upset about it going out in the wrong shoes. And without a hat on.

We went back into town and I asked Roger if he wanted to come home and see the flat. He said he would love to. We went to the flat. Three minutes later we were in my bedroom, falling on the bed, as I told him I didn't have any knickers on, and had been like that all day.

La la la la la la la la la la la la la la la la la la la la, went all the birds in Yorkshire and a nightingale sang in Millennium Square. Which is in Leeds, dear southern and foreign readers.

I will skip quickly past the lovely details because you will only get all hot and bothered if I give you a blow by blow account, also it would take up too much space and there are so many other things I need you to know about. I'm sure you know lots about sex. If you don't, there are lots of good books on the subject. I can particularly recommend the ones for teenagers which are delightfully frank and no-nonsense. Especially on techniques for blowjobs. Particularly the one Nancy has. (I didn't realise quite how explicit it was when I bought it, but I learnt a tip or two I don't mind telling you.) So let's just say it was fabulous and leave it at that.

Roger and I parted (after he had taken me, post-coitally, to dinner in the best restaurant we could get into at short-notice) on excessively devoted terms and with many promises to see each other soon. Hoorah! I was an adulteress and I had a proper boyfriend!

However, I may be MAD but I'm not STUPID as I believe I have mentioned. (Please insert your own family motto which gives you hope and encouragement when times are hard at this point.)

Consequently, being realistic, I thought that it was quite possible that I would never see Roger again, I was prepared for it and so was surprised and pleased when he rang the next day to tell me how fabulous I was.

"Can I see you on Tuesday?"

"Oh no, I'm afraid not, that's impossible, I have to go to Nancy's parent's evening. Or rather I suppose they expect parents's evening but they will be disappointed."

This went straight over his head, being an inaudible pun. Luckily he ignored it.

"There's a good production on at the Playhouse - got a wonderful review in the paper, and -"

Oh my God, I thought, and he likes the theatre! This is too good to be true!

"Another night would be lovely," I interrupted with only a slight tremor of regret, "but definitely not Tuesday."

"What a shame."

"Yes."

"I'll check my diary and have a rethink."

He went. Possibly to check his diary, or more probably to cross me off his list because I was too unavailable. Oh well. I would always put Nancy first, no matter what. Never mind Jolly Roger. If he couldn't understand about my devotion to my daughter I wouldn't be able to go out with him anyway. And just when I had fallen in love with him, like an idiot! But I hadn't liked the note of disapproval in his voice, like the teacher who feels you have let him down by giving the wrong answer when he was counting on you to know that the Ghost of Hamlet's father represented poison and disease and you said that the ghost popping up like that reminded you of Mr Punch and you thought it was a metaphor for his lost childhood.

Thus I was thinking about my own studies and how much I had hated my school (of course, they had totally failed to understand my sensitive yet intransigent nature) as I carefully chose my attire for parent's evening. So vital not to let down one's child by looking a) frumpy or b) tarty. Unfortunately I had very few clothes which fell into neither of these categories, but I found a sort of woollen overshirt which looked acceptable with jeans and a vest top. I put my ankle boots on again because the sound they made, clopping along the corridors, gave me the illusion of being in control of the situation. I also wore an oversized turquoise necklace, bought by me and for me on holiday on Turkey against the advice of my former husband who said it was a waste of money. Ha! It was my first parent's evening on my own. Everyone else was a couple. I knew some of them, of course, they were the parents of Nancy's friends, and they were warily nice to me, as if I had cancer or my child had died and they were afraid I would suddenly rend my garments and wail. We all sat about on seats in a holding area awaiting our turn, watching like hawks for people trying to push in.

"Are you here to see Mr Birch?"

"No, I thought this was the queue for the cheese counter." Eventually I got to see Nancy's English teacher Mr Birch (Graeme Birch it said on a sign on his desk) and sat down self-consciously alone and not part of a couple like everyone else.

"I'm very worried about Nancy," he said.

"But she's working so hard," I exclaimed, alarmed to hear someone say something semi-negative about Nancy for the first time in her entire school career. Nancy had always been the perfect baby, toddler, small child, large child and adolescent.

"I think she's working too hard," he said, looking me earnestly in the eye. He was a stocky, darkish young man in his early thirties, much too young for me, quite attractive in a Dylan Thomas sort of way.

"But you know she wants to do English A level -"

"Oh, there'll be no problem with that, I assure you - er - Mrs -"

"Holly."

"I think these results might not reflect her true potential, er, Holly, to be honest with you. I think the, er, breakup may have brought her down in a couple of places. The fact is that Nancy is an exceptionally capable young woman and the overworking is tiring her out to the extent that she is not performing at her highest level. But I don't want you to worry-"

Too late for that!

"- I don't think it will affect the way universities view her application, if we explain the er, extenuating circumstances."

Oh God! Nancy was going to fail in her ambition to do medicine and it would be all my fault for failing to hold my marriage together!

"But what if they don't take any notice? What if they think we're just whinging and making excuses? Middle-class moaners - why would they listen to that?"

"Nancy's record speaks for itself, er, Holly. Even if there is a blip - and we don't have her results yet, they might be fine - but even if they're not, we can explain it away."

"Well I'm really worried now."

Chapter 5. Opening the Hangar Doors

"I didn't mean to worry you, Mrs, er, Holly, I just wanted to reassure you that we will be doing everything we can to help Nancy to succeed in what she wants to achieve," he said taking off his glasses and looking at me with such an expression of what I can only describe as doggy begging that I kind of felt sorry for him.

"I'm sure you're doing your best."

"Oh I am," he said fervently. "I want the absolute best for all our er, pupils. And Nancy is so exceptional that I see her as a, er, special case, given the er, circumstances."

"It's very nice of you to care so much," I said, "but I do think that she's going to be fine, if everyone gives her a bit of space."

Chemistry, maths, biology and physics didn't seem to be too worried about Nancy, and they were the important ones after all, so after I'd seen them I started to relax a bit. French was a series of despairing Martine-style shrugs from the assistant, but that may have been because I tried to speak French to her, and Nancy always did well in French so I ignored it. Then I met the deputy head, who was Nancy's form tutor. Her name was Miss Bligh, and she always cheered me up because she was seriously eccentric in her choice of clothing. Today she was sporting a gold lurex tank top, a white pleated knee length skirt, gold platform sandals and a nautical jacket, accessorized with large gold anchor-shaped earrings and a tremendous number of large brass bangles which clanked every time she moved, which was all the time. Miss Bligh is at least sixty and probably more, though I don't like to ask. Surely she should have retired by now.

"I'm so worried about Nancy," Miss Bligh began, failing to beat about the bush.

"Not you too! Why, Miss Bligh? She's been more or less - well, at home she's been a bit odd actually. Grumpy. Uncommunicative."

"Exactly. That's what I have here too, my normally bright, chatty Nancy has become a little black cloud in our midst. So gloomy. The poor child."

She sat forward in her seat and put her hand over mine on the table. "I'm afraid she's taking this separation very badly."

"It's not a separation, it's a divorce," I said a little too firmly and several people looked our way.

"I think Nancy believes there may be a little ray of hope," said Miss Bligh in a way that I suspect was tremulous.

"There is NO ray of hope, Miss Bligh. Au contraire, the thing is so tightly sealed against hope that it may begin to generate antimatter, or antihope, of its own accord, as it is to hope what a black hole is to the universe." (I was fresh from talking to the physics teacher).

"I see. Poor Nancy. I think she loves you both, you see."

"I know she does. That's how it is. It's tough. I'm expecting the school to be very understanding and supportive."

"Oh we ARE!" Miss Bligh exclaimed.

"Good. Like, for example, when she comes to apply to universities?" "Of COURSE, we always do what we can, but the fact is that children always do better when their parents stay together for better or for worse."

"Hmmm."

"I hope you are considering mediation?"

Look, I didn't come here for counselling, lady, I wanted to say, but decided to take a deep breath and count to ten instead. I smiled and stood up.

"Thank you so much for your concern, Miss Bligh. Let's both do our bit to get her through these horrible exams, shall we, and worry about other things another time."

I picked up my bag, and prepared to depart.

"But - there are so many tips I wanted to give you on how to keep your man!" Miss Bligh exclaimed, rather loudly, and this time the entire hall looked in our direction.

"Another time, Miss Bligh, another time."

I fled the building.

"Honestly, Carla," I said as we sipped our giant glasses of wine two days later in the Frog and Peach, "it was humiliating."

"You should have told her to shove her advice where the rays of hope don't shine," said Carla and we laughed a bit longer than the joke deserved, because we were already a bit tiddly, and it was only eight o'clock.

"Little black cloud!" said Carla when we stopped laughing, and so we set off again.

"I know, it's so politically incorrect too. I thought teachers had to go on courses about that, these days. How appalling!"

We were starting to attract attention from other customers in the pub with our geriatric cackling. It was quite a nice pub - possibly a bit too nice. There were a lot of earnest twenty-something couples holding hands and having fierce rows in hushed tones, I guessed because they had moved in together and couldn't decide what colour towels to have. I surmised that he wanted purple, because it doesn't show the dirt so quickly, but she wanted peach, because you can get matching toilet paper. "Have you ever seen purple toilet paper?" she was probably hissing, which was why she was looking so furious. They both knew they were right, and the row would go on until they got to the cinema, be put on hold while they watched the film, and then resume again in the car home. With luck, it could be one they could bring out and use over and over again for the next ten years. "Look at the skid mark on this towel! How could you be so gross?" "Well I did tell you to get purple you daft cow. It wouldn't've showed on a purple towel, would it?"

Thinking about this I missed Carla's next remarks and had to ask her to repeat them.

"I said, that man over there is looking at us."

"Well he needn't look at me," I said cheerfully, "I have an official boyfriend."

"Oh yes, the one who hasn't rung back yet."

"He will ring back - he's just checking his diary."

"Oh yes. I think he's been checking his diary for four days now? Is he a very slow reader?"

"In any case," I said firmly, "you can have the chap over there."

I looked at him for the first time and recognised the man who had been in the pub the first time I had gone out with Carla, the stocky chap in the brown leather jacket. He had been watching Carla then, and now he was watching her again.

"I've seen him before! He's stalking you, Carla!"

She laughed. "Milltown is a small place and there are only a few pubs to go to, it's not surprising to see the same people sometimes. But I think you are right and maybe I have seen him before. Maybe I will go and talk to him."

She stood up and crossed the bar, before I could suggest that I came too. I saw her speak to the man. He put down his pint, looked surprised and then said something to her. They had a short conversation, Carla waving her hands about a lot, but then she always did, even when she was talking about Martine or seasonal herbs (as she had been before we got onto Nancy's parents' evening.) Then Carla came back to our table, and the man left the pub.

"That was a bit of a risky thing to do!"

She shrugged. "There are plenty of people in here, so no danger. He says he thought he knows me from somewhere, I say I don't think so, he decided to leave. That's it!"

I felt there was more going on here than Carla was telling me. However, at this moment I got a text message, which entirely distracted me. It was from Roger, and said: need to c u sat, urgent.

"Don't answer it straight away", Carla said, "make him wait." But I couldn't wait, though I did manage thirty seconds before texting back: ok.

"You are hopeless, Holly," Carla said. "And you say this man wants a baby? What is that to do with you? You have a teenager - why would you want a baby?"

"I don't want one - but I am still capable of reproducing, you know. In theory." My phone rang, it was Roger.

"Hello," he said, "you got my text then."

"Yes."

"Are you at home?" His tone was low and seductive.

"No, actually, er, I'm out in a pub with Carla. You know, the friend from work. Called Carla."

"I remember," he said vaguely. "OK. Do you go out to pubs a lot?"

"Well, more recently, since I've been, er, on my own with Nancy. Need to give her a bit of space, er, et cetera. Is it a problem?"

"Not at all. Not at all. Well, can I see you on Saturday?"

"That would be lovely."

"I'll pick you up at eight."

"OK."

"Goodnight."

"Goodnight."

"That didn't go too well," Carla said. She seemed almost pleased about it.

"No, it was a bit weird."

"I think this man is bad for you."

"Well he's nicer than that usually. I felt kind of in the wrong somehow."

"But you're not in the wrong," said Carla decisively. "I will get us another drink to show we are not in the wrong."

When she came back to the table with the drinks I went back to our earlier conversation.

"So I should be planting basil now?" I asked.

"You can't get the right flavour if it's not fresh. And those supermarket pots are not good, forced, and sooooo expensive."

"I'll do it. And it will remind me of my solicitor the lovely Basil, who is so good and reliable but I haven't heard from him for a while."

"Is he expecting a settlement soon?" Carla asked, sitting forward a little.

"I don't think so. I think he's expecting to go to court unless we do something drastic."

"I, too, am hoping for a settlement not too far away," Carla sighed.

"Really? From your divorce?"

"Yes. I have been informed that the papers are in order at last, and proceedings can begin. Unfortunately as I am in a foreign country I will have to find several hundreds, if not thousands of pounds to commence." She took a desolate drag of her Silk Cut.

"But when I get my settlement I'll be able to lend you some," I exclaimed.

"I won't let you, don't be so silly," Carla said quickly.

"Well I can't right now, anyway, because I haven't got it, but when I do I'll make sure I lend you what you need to get your rights too. Hey! Sisterhood of the Divorced!"

"You are a very sweet person, you know," Carla said, "but I can't let you do that. Thank you for thinking of me." And she kissed me on the cheek, arousing the interest of several men at adjoining tables, who had to be sharply recalled to attention by their women.

Chapter 6

After dinner bint

I was back at work (with a slight headache, not improved by Martine booming in my headphones - yes, by an evil twist of fate she was my supervisor again.) I was three people today. I was the Aston Martin information hotline, in both English and French, the Yorkshire Dales cottage redirection desk, and the Fabulous Waxed Jackets help line.

So technically four people. There were very few calls for the last one. Most of the calls were for cottages, which was dull, as I only redirected them most of the time, and which flashed up as 3 on screen when the phone rang. I had to pick up within three rings, know who I was supposed to be, and be armed with the correct info. And speaking the right language. I didn't always get it right.

"Bonjour, information Aston Martin whoops I mean Yorkshire Dales cottages how can I help?"

Usually when I messed up Martine was listening in.

"Olly! That is the sixth time. I am keeping score. Please pay more attention. It is very simple, you need to just look on the screen to see who is calling. I think anyone can understand this. Even a very stupid person I think."

But the trouble was, unlike dialling out, when I knew when it was coming, all these incoming calls were scattered around like knickers on a teenager's bedroom floor, unpredictable, and, almost invariably, unwelcome. It was nearing the end of the day, I was tiring, when this amazing thing happened:

"Hello - er - wotsit - Aston Martin information, how can I help you?"

"I need a part." It was a deep, familiar, Yorkshire voice. "She's broken down and I need this bit - I found the serial number - it's SN71002539PZ212. Do you have it in stock?"

I failed to interrupt the voice to tell him I wasn't a stockist of parts because there was something fabulous about it - something that made me shiver as if someone had walked over my grave.

"I can give you telephone numbers," I said rather less than helpfully, "but I don't carry a list of parts, I'm sorry. If you can tell me a little more about yourself I can redirect you to your nearest stockist."

"Well, alright then." He sounded a bit displeased.

"Can I have your full name please?"

"Steve Harley."

I was startled. My thoughts collected themselves and settled into a pattern I could recognise.

"The Steve Harley?"

He laughed. It was a lovely laugh. "Not the one out of Cockney Rebel, no. Though obviously, there's a resemblance... but I'm not as old as him."

"No - I didn't mean that." I said, eagerly. "I meant - the Steve Harley I was at school with."

"I was at school with a lot of people."

"Windy Hill Primary?"

"Yes?" His voice had gone a bit tense.

"This is Holly Field."

There was a silence at the end of the line.

"Hello Holly. Wow - how about that - I used to have a bit of a crush on you."

It was my turn to go quiet.

"I didn't know that."

"Oh aye."

"Well, and I thought we were just good mates letting off bangers inside bits of scaffolding with milk bottles on the end."

"Hey, you remember that?"

"Well considering the risk of blinding for life, yes, curiously enough I do."

"It was good fun, though, wasn't it?"

"Adrenaline charged."

"We were eleven. It's an exciting age."

"I liked it."

"How are you?"

"Little changed in the fear of blinding department, but a bit older generally."

"I bet you aren't."

"Well obviously in some ways I will always be eleven. The bit of me that likes wandering about in half-built houses in the dark for example. Not that I do much of that, these days. I think it's illegal, now. You'd get an ASBO."

"What do you do these days? That's legal?"

"I work in a call centre. As you may have noticed."

"Oh, aye? How come?"

"You know - life's rich tapestry and all that."

"I see. Go on."

"Holly!" Martine's voice broke in. "I don't think you are in the script?"

"Sorry, Martine, I -"

The line had gone dead. Martine had cut us off. I was devastated. Steve Harley! He was gone. Oh my God. I sat staring at the screen in disbelief, but happily it was only seconds before the phone rang again.

"Oh - Steve?"

"I have a problem with my new jacket and I'm hoping you can sort it for me," said a very posh voice indeed.

"Oh God! I'm sorry. I see. Yes."

"This is Lady Georgina Crackpot," or something, the voice went on even more annoyingly, "I bought the jacket in my local shop, Hacking Toffs, but imagine my annoyance when I found that my friend Henrietta had bought exactly the same jacket twenty pounds cheaper on an internet web thing. I went back to Hacking Toffs and _"

"Yes, yes," I interrupted, "I think you'll find that pricing policy is at the discretion of the retailer. Now could we wrap this call up as someone rather important is trying to get through."

"Well really!" Lady Georgina exploded, "of all the insolent, obnoxious, ill-bred half wits!"

"I couldn't have put it better myself," I said, hanging up and praying that Martine had failed to notice.

She hadn't.

"It is the end of the day, and the phones are closed," she added pointedly, "or I would tell you to leave early. As it is I don't expect to see you tomorrow, or ever here again as long as I am here."

"That's fine with me, Martine, because if I ever see you and your annoying pointy French nose again I may have to flatten it, and you. Au revoir."

"Is zat a sreat?" she was shouting after me as I stomped out. Her accent had gone much more French than usual.

But I didn't really care about any of that, because I had been talking to my old mate Steve Harley - ah, the golden days of yore - with Steve I played conkers, I fished, I sledged and I made dodgy swings over rather grimy becks. At his house, his mum once let us make a jug of shandy and when she wasn't looking he tipped the whole bottle of beer in. That afternoon passed in a bit of a blur at the bottom of his garden surrounded by delphiniums and phlox. We made whole worlds out of, if not a grain, at least a huge great builder's heap of sand. Then we grew up - sort of, in my case - and I was sent to a school that my parents hoped would get rid of the unfortunate Yorkshire accent. The end of childhood. Life, eh?

My mother rang me that night.

"Hello dear, I hope you're well? I'm super, except for a bit of a twinge when it's cold and wet, like it is at the moment, makes it a bit tricky to drive, otherwise I'd come and give you a hand" (there was no real danger of this, thankfully) "I'd love to see you, as it happens, I brought you back a lovely prayer rug from Nepal, I got several actually because I thought what super cushion covers they would make, I gave one to Amanda and she's made one already, she's such a clever girl, and I started making one myself because, as it happens, you know that lemon blouse? You know, that one I got in Marshall's when it was still Marshall's which shows what a long time ago it was? Must be twenty, maybe thirty years. What is it now, house of Fraser or some such thing? What's that then? How time goes by, I can hardly bear it. I think it's Viyella, anyway I wore it with everything, it went so well with pinnies and slacks. Well I was out pruning the Golden Shower over the garage - you know, that yellow rambler, and the wretched thing tore the sleeve! I was so upset, my lovely lemon blouse! I've had it for thirty years, and it's such good quality. You can't get that kind of quality now you know. It was such a bad tear. But, as I say, Amanda was over, with the children, she's such a good daughter-in-law, you know how clever she is, she said it wasn't possible to repair it, she had a good look, and so she cut out a piece for the back of the cushion cover from the remains! I can't thank her enough. She didn't manage to finish sewing it, because she had to dash off, but I've been struggling with my arthritic old fingers to complete her handiwork, ha ha ha! Well it's been lovely to talk to you, dear, and to hear that you're coping so well, of course I knew you would because you always land on your feet, don't you? You're a coper, I always tell people who ask about you, Holly is such a coper. She always copes. I hope you manage to make it down here to see your old mum one of these days. I must dash, people coming for bridge and I must put out the nibbles. Bye, dear."

Which was comforting.

On Saturday, Roger came and picked me up. He met Nancy in the process. She scowled at him, but said very little. He put himself out to be charming, asking her about her musical tastes and keeping off the subject of exams. He was driving a very sexy car which he hadn't been driving last time I met him. It wasn't an Aston Martin, though. Even so I politely admired it as I got in.

"New car?"

"Er - yes, I got it this week."

"It's lovely."

"Thanks."

There was a slight pause.

"Do you like my new shoes?" I said.

"Wow, yes!"

"That's all right then."

"We've both been trying to impress," Roger said after a short silence.

"Yes, that's good isn't it?"

"I'm a bit smitten with you, you know."

"Me too."

There was another silence as we contemplated what we had just said.

"I hope you'll like the restaurant I've chosen."

"I'm sure I will."

Actually I was terribly disappointed. Going in I was impressed. It looked fabulous and was in a nice bit of the otherwise horrid town where Roger chose to live. Why Roger chose to live there was a mystery to me, as most men in his exalted position preferred nice bits of Leeds or one of its satellite nice towns (like lovely lovely Morton Spa). The dining experience went wrong quite quickly. The waiters were fussy, and the maitre d' accidentally brushed her ballpoint pen against my suede coat (but I didn't notice until I got home). The menu was pretentious, the bread was dry, the house wine was acid and the coffee, when it finally arrived, had been sitting around all evening turning sour with boredom. I had the fillet steak, I was starving, (Nancy would have been so jealous) and it was fine, but the vegetables were soggy. He had swordfish. It looked dreary.

"How's your fish?"

"Fine. How was your week?"

"Oh, it was good, mostly. Parents' evening was a bit of a disaster. It's very tricky adapting to be a single parent. How was yours?"

"Fine, but boring. How I envy you your family life."

"I quite envy you your peace and quiet," I chuckled but Roger didn't even smile.

"I really do want children," he sighed.

"Yes, but, I'm so old -"

"Not old at all." Bless his kindly heart. Mind you, he was the same age as me. So probably didn't think it was very old.

What was it? Looking back I can't entirely explain why I was so desperately in love with Roger. The sex was fabulous, and after all those years of marriage (and childbirth) it was rather marvellous to find out what it was all about, really. He was clever and funny and we were highly attuned to one another. We liked a lot of the same things. Then, he took me sailing; a major childhood fantasy came true.

"Would you like to come on holiday with me?"

I had been gazing at my plate, thinking what a pity it was not to finish my dinner, but that I really didn't want to eat it, so I shouldn't, but on the other hand it was a shocking waste of food, with millions of people starving, but if I wasn't hungry any more I was just being greedy, which was bad, and then I might get fat, which would be dreadful. You know.

That conversation. Suddenly it was driven from my mind.

"Gosh, yes."

"I thought a week sailing in the Hebrides."

"Er - wow." What could I say? Until he said that, the word holiday had meant beach, sun, towel, book, sun cream. (Plus seafood and sex, in the evenings, obviously).

"How soon can you get away?"

"Er -"

"Is next week too soon?"

"Er -"

"I'll book something."

"OK. Gosh. Er - just like that." My Tommy Cooper impression lacked conviction.

"You like eating your food," he said, changing the subject abruptly in a way he was wont to do, sounding slightly disapproving, or possibly deeply excited.

"I think you can tell a lot about people from the way they eat," I said, keeping on eating.

"Elaborate?"

"Well," I said with my mouth full, "for example, do they go at it with greedy relish or nibble at the edges? Dancing can be a good indicator, too. I may not be good at body language, but I can see when someone's a good dancer. You know, that's why I mentioned eating and dancing in my ad."

"Hmmm. You haven't seen me dancing."

"Do I want to? When I've seen you eating."

"And?"

"You eat like you make love."

"Mmmmm."

It got a bit steamy after that, as you can imagine (I hope you're committing these invaluable steam-generating lines to heart), and we adjourned shortly afterwards to his place.

By the way - possibly I should have spelled it out earlier, when I mentioned the sex books - on the subject of sex - I may need to explain, to anyone who finds herself in my position, that sex has changed since you got married twenty years ago. All kinds of stuff which was rather outre then is now standard practice. You may find it a bit yucky at first, but trust me, if you just go for it, cast aside your inhibitions, you'll find that most of it is quite fun - with the right person. Or actually, even with the wrong person.

I liked Roger's place (and indeed doing rather outre things with him in bed; and other places) but he explained to me that it was rented and he was intending to buy when he found exactly the right house. It occurred to me that this was perfect because I wanted to buy somewhere too, and if we were getting on so well in, say, six months' time we could pool resources.

I really needed to curb my tendency to imagine the perfect life with every new man I met. I had it all worked out with Roger - the house, the second house, the holidays, the yacht... But I was getting the message that Roger wasn't in the pooling anything department, as he made all his own decisions. He was a one-man reality check. Maybe I would still buy a house in France. Just in case (in the highly unlikely event that) it didn't work out.

Nancy was not thrilled when I said I was going on holiday with Roger. Her exams were nearly over, and she was planning a week of riot with her friends in any case, but the prospect of me bunking off with Roger was not pleasing to her.

"I don't know why, but I don't trust him," she said eventually.

"You're feeling threatened," I said patiently, "of course you don't like me to have a new man in my life. But it doesn't change our relationship -"

"Oh, skip the patronising self-help claptrap," she shouted impatiently, "have you listened to yourself? You sound like bloody Jerry Springer! Mindless TV pop psychology! I do not feel threatened, I just don't think he's right for you and there's something about him that creeps me out. That's all."

Oh dear. She really was feeling threatened.

The following day, Nancy did her last GCSE. She came home looking washed out but after a bath she came downstairs in her (My Little Pony) pyjamas and (Little Miss Naughty) dressing gown looking more fabulous than ever, her skin glowing and her eyes like sunlight through toffee. She smelled fabulous too (was that my precious and dwindling stock of extremely expensive soap, left over from my former life?)

"You're not going out to celebrate tonight?"

"No, we're all going out at the weekend. Jess and Freya still have German tomorrow."

"What shall we do tonight?"

"Let's watch a girlie DVD. Bridget Jones, or Pride and Prejudice."

"I wish they'd make a film of Northanger Abbey - that's my

favourite - I particularly like the bit where the fat ugly guy is banging on about carriages and horses the way men these days go on about cars. Jane Austen is so nasty."

"I can read Northanger Abbey now I'm not going exams any more! I can read anything I like!" Nancy cried joyfully and we danced round the room like maniacs until I knocked a lamp over.

I cooked her favourite food (bangers and mash, with the bangers stuck in the mash, cartoon-style; sauce rouge ou brun) and, over a bottle of red wine, I nervously told her about Goodfun Productions and the dream house in France. To my extreme amazement, she was interested, even keen.

"What, you mean we get a free holiday?"

"Well, yes, but we have to go round these houses and say what we think of them. On film. But of course, no-one needs to know, after all, nobody watches those programmes apart from very old people. Hence the advert breaks for walk-in baths and ear drops."

"I think it sounds fun."

"You do? Er - I mean - yes, of course it will be."

"Will there be hunky cameramen?"

"I think they're standard issue."

"Let's go for it! Anyway, it would be cool if you lived in France, I could come and stay. Would Roger live with you?"

"Probably not." I said cautiously. "Er -"

"What?"

"Where would you live if I was in France?"

"With dad, I guess."

"I guess...."

Ooh, I hadn't thought of that. Nevertheless, I contacted Goodfun Productions and we arranged a screen test. I decided not to mention it to Roger.

That night we watched Jean de Florette. I hoped it wasn't an omen.

Chapter 7

The Great Wen

Nancy and I went to London for our screen test by train. Nancy was wearing a tiny little top and a tiny little skirt which failed, in a mother's eyes, to cover her adequately. In fact she looked fantastic, and attracted attention from men of all ages. After a great deal of agonising about fashion, I was wearing linen trousers and a jersey top. We zoomed down through England on our intercity train with our noses glued to the window, like six year olds on a school trip. She saw a buzzard near Doncaster and I saw a heron, flapping so slowly over Warwickshire that it appeared to be in danger of losing momentum and plummeting to earth. Just outside Hatfield we both saw great crested grebes on a flooded gravel pit, to our great and noisy delight and to the extreme irritation of the rest of the carriage. Even I could tell that we were getting on their nerves, as everyone, even the old people, turned up their i-pods so loud that we could (and did, noisily) identify the tunes. We ate sandwiches we had brought from home, clementines, bananas and chocolate cake (made by Nancy to celebrate end-of-exams) and scattered our debris all over the table, to the loudly expressed disgust of our neighbours. We didn't care. We arrived in London in a state of childlike excitement which was fuelled by a taxi ride during which we spotted Big

Ben and the London Eye. We were grating on the nerves of the taxi driver when we arrived at the (rather disappointing) headquarters of Goodfun but we remained high on life all through the interview process and consequently made a good impression. Of course! Television loves people like us. It's just in real life that people find us a bit eccentric. And annoying.

They were based in the East End, in warehouse premises that weren't modernised to the standards I'd seen in lifestyle magazines. In fact it reminded me of less attractive bits of Sad City. A former industrial site, it was now a place for new enterprise. The people who worked there did not slave in sweatshops like their unlucky predecessors, but had super jobs in the media. They were uniformly charming but seemed only to be there because they were related to someone who knew someone who knew daddy. In fact it was possible that they were all related to each other in an alarming inbreeding experiment.

"Oh yah! No way! Awesome!" they continually shouted to each other, as they sat at their computer screens or swanked across the huge open-plan office in the sort of clothes noone normal would dream of wearing in Yorkshire.

We were interviewed by Helena, who flicked her hair back every twenty seconds and for whom no remark was tactless.

"So, Holly, you're a single mum now..."

"Yes."

"What's it like then, being a single mum?"

"Oh, you know, sort of the same as being a non-single mum."

"But is it much harder?"

"Well, it means I have to do all the driving."

"Spectacular! What fun! You're doing great! Look at Nancy!"

"Yes, I'm very proud."

"So, Nancy, you just did your exams?"

"Yes."

"No way, I'm soooo in awe of you, Nancy! I was soooo stupid at school. So, what do you think about your mum moving to France? Won't you miss her? I mean, my mum's in Martinique and that's awesome. Mind you, I don't get there as much as I'd like. And she never gets over here, what with her business and all. But she's waaaaay cool."

"How old are you, Helena?"

"I'm twenty," Helena said, rather sadly I thought.

"I think your mum should come and see you," I said decisively, "if you like I'll ring her and tell her. What's her number in Martinique?"

For a few seconds, Helena seemed to be thinking about the possibility of this, before she shook her hair back again, firmly readjusted her hairband and said:

"Sweet of you, really sweet, but we must get on."

"But I still think I should talk to your mother. Tell her what's what. Mother to mother."

"Right. We're not doing that. Back to the interview, alright, yah? What's the position with your own property?"

"Ah."

This was, of course, the tricky question.

"My house is sold" (that bit was true) "but the funds haven't come through just yet."

Nancy shot me a look which I failed to interpret.

"So you're not in a position to buy at this moment?"

"Not today," I said carefully, "but by the time we film I expect to be."

"OK, sweet, I'll see what the producer thinks. If you just wait here a sec, I'll pop along and show her your tape. I'm sure she'll be thrilled. She might even pop along and check you out."

She did indeed pop along shortly afterwards, accompanied by a breathless Helena, and looked us up and down in a manner which reminded me of Martine. Our producer, whose name I only learnt later, from the programme credits, as she failed to introduce herself, was as thin as the so-called women in the transvestite bar in Leeds, but more tastefully dressed in mostly beige floppy garments. She clearly approved of Nancy and focussed on her her huge brown eyes and all her attention. Nancy basked.

"What a very beautiful girl, how lovely for the film crews to have someone so charming to film, what eyes, what hair, usually we have middle-aged couples who are not exactly photogenic. Have you thought about modelling?"

"Of course she hasn't," I interrupted, "she's a very serious girl and she wants to be a doctor."

"But I could still be a model in the holidays," Nancy said quickly.

"No you couldn't!"

"Yes I could!"

"Don't be ridiculous!"

The producer fell silent, watching us with a little smile on her face.

"I'm not being ridiculous, mother, it's you - you don't know what you're talking about."

"Alright," I said smoothly. "I'm sorry."

Nancy looked astounded at this capitulation, as well she might, because it was purely for show: because I didn't want to provide any more entertainment for the producer than I was contracted for. I would make sure to tell Nancy exactly what I thought on the train home. In explicit detail. As we were leaving, however, I thought I saw Helena slip a card to Nancy, and I was filled with sudden fear. Was it safe to let Nancy out? Especially as, the minute she set foot in London, people were asking her if she wanted to be a model? As I had long suspected, she was clearly far too pretty. I needed to get her back to Yorkshire, lecturing her on the way.

On the train home, though, I was distracted by a phone call from Basil.

"I despair of your soon to be ex-husband, Mrs Meansod."

"Holly, please - or Ms Field."

"Sorry, Miss Field, of course."

I sighed.

"He simply won't play the game. We are going to have to be a bit crafty with him."

"Oh?"

"I propose to instruct counsel," said Basil, sounding as if he might explode with suppressed excitement.

"Er - what exactly does that mean?"

"It means that you and I are going to visit a barrister and ask his opinion, and if necessary, take him with us to court."

"Gosh, won't that be a bit expensive? I mean, you hear about fees -"

"Yes, yes, of course it would be expensive if we were to actually go through with it. Mr Meansod would have to have his own counsel and the costs would be astronomic. I imagine that Mr M will want to avoid that, as we will be applying for costs. It would add several thousand pounds to his bill, as I am sure his solicitor will explain to him."

"I see. I think. It's a bluff. Ooh, Basil, are we playing games with the law? Isn't that a bit dodgy?"

"It is a bluff, but it is not "dodgy", as you call it. I will be glad to have the opinion of my learned friend. I hope in a couple of weeks we will have your money. In the meantime, I need you to come with me to Leeds on Wednesday afternoon, will that be convenient?"

What with all this gadding about and spending money instead of earning it, things were getting a bit tight again. Roger had gone away for a few days and I wasn't being taken out for lovely meals any more, Nancy was at home all day, eating expensive food, and my sister had finally realised that I was on my own and had decided that she needed to come and sort me out.

"No, Jane, you can't come and stay. I can't afford to put you up."

"I'll stay in a B&B."

"No, really, you can't. I won't let you. It's not that I don't want to see you" (it was that I didn't want to see her) "it's just that everything is so complicated at the moment that I can't cope with -"

"I'll see you on the 20th," my sister said, and rang off.

"That's all I need," I said to Nancy.

"I like Aunty Jane," she said.

"I like her too, but I can't afford to feed her," looking meaningfully at Nancy's overflowing plate of toast and jam.

"I've got a job, actually," she announced. "Two jobs, in fact. So I'll be able to afford my own toast."

"No need to be sarcastic. What's the job - er - jobs? Not modelling?" I said feeling a nasty tight panic forming in my chest.

"I'm working in the hardware shop in town."

"What, hammers and screwdrivers? You don't know a thing about any of that!"

"I'll get training."

"What's the other job?"

"Oh," said Nancy thickly through a mouthful of toast so large that a blob of bilberry jam (my own, last year's - how long ago it seemed when Nancy and I had picked the bilberries on a sunny afternoon and seen a merlin) - escaped from the corner of her mouth and fell, fortunately for her, on the plate below. "Babysitting."

"Honestly, you nearly got jam on the carpet."

"I did not. I was very careful."

"If you didn't stuff so much in your mouth - I can't believe how greedy you are, Nancy."

"Isn't it time you got ready for the barrister?"

"Oh crikey, yes, what shall I wear? Do I want to look downtrodden or sassy? How do I play this?"

"Downtrodden. Mess your hair up, and streak your mascara as if you've been sobbing uncontrollably. Oh, no need, you already look like that."

"Sarcastic. Unhelpful."

I needn't have worried, anyway, because the barrister was only, as Basil put it, a shot across the bows. Basil had got a glint in his eye and a spring in his step these days from being my admiral in twinkling epaulettes. I could imagine him running a certain someone through with his cutlass, or was it pirates who did that? Basil and I had a lovely drive into Leeds, a lovely time with the lovely barrister (who told Basil to just carry on as he was going) and a lovely drive back after a lovely cup of coffee.

"Everything is going to be fine, Holly," Basil said, as we purred along in his rather gorgeous and expensive car (which was not, however, an Aston Martin). The Brahms requiem was playing, rather unnecessarily gloomily, in the background as we sped through pretty bits of Yorkshire. Basil explained that his wife's choral society were to perform it at their next concert, and that it was on in the car so that she could learn her part. It didn't seem even slightly like an omen. The weather had improved slightly, as we approached midsummer, and occasionally the sun came out and transformed everything, as it was doing now, as if to reinforce Basil's optimism in a pathetic fallacy kind of way. Soon we would be able to go bilberry picking again. Everything was going to be fine. Honestly.

Chapter 8

Dancing the blanket hornpipe

I bought a lot of very rustly clothes to take to Scotland with me, including rustly waterproof trousers which were desperately unflattering, but I needn't have bothered, because we were blessed with lovely weather and I never wore them. Most of the time I wore a bikini, apart from one memorable day.

We arrived at the quayside after a rather fraught car journey during which Roger, to my noisy distress, hit a pheasant and got blood all over his number plate; and we had a very nasty meal at a roadside café. ("I knew we should have scraped up that pheasant!" Yes, but who would have cooked it? Exactly.)

The boat was waiting for us in the small harbour, pulling gently but insistently at her rope as if she was impatient to be off. Small islands were blue on the horizon, like dreams. We boarded. Which is the technical term for getting on. I was terribly excited. It was like a Wendy house only floating, and with an engine, and sails. And lots of ropes. ("Yards, Holly¡‘) There were sofas and bedrooms and a teeny weeny bathroom (head). There was a microscopic kitchen, (galley) but an enormous table (for charts, which are what landlubbers call maps). We were given instructions about the equipment and how to use it, the best places to stop for the night, and how to call for help in an emergency. I was so excited I ran up and down the deck like a puppy.

"Can I just say help? Or is there a technical term I should be aware of? Like SOS, mayday, we are foundering with all hands?"

Rather too quickly for my liking, we set off. I was all at sea. With Roger. Alone. We sailed from the Kyle of somewhere to the Bute of somewhere else, I think, but don't ask me about the route, as I was too busy worrying. Not worrying about anything specifically, just worrying in general. The whole business was alarming. Roger was (literally) in his element. I realised, after about ten minutes of sailing away, that I didn't trust the sea.

It was almost unbearably beautiful. The sea began by being well-behaved and sped from our prow in little waves, fringed with white like crocheted baby blankets. At night, the same little waves were fringed with phosphorescence. There was just enough wind to ensure that we didn't need to use the engine, but just drifted along under sail. It wasn't really fast enough for Roger.

The islands were all shapes and sizes, from alarmingly over-risen ones like giant loaves of bread with beetling cliffs covered in seabirds, to islands so flat and so almost entirely made of beach they seemed in danger of being washed away by the incoming tide. Sometimes we stopped and rowed ashore in the dinghy, but mostly we just sailed by under the endlessly blue skies.

My main job (apart from all housekeeping activities, but obviously that doesn't count as a Real Boat Job) was to be In Charge of the Anchor. At first, I thought this was a good thing, because it meant I only had things to do at the stopping and starting bits of our voyage, but then I cottoned on that Roger wasn't doing that much (apart from setting our course on the computer and letting the autopilot steer, then sitting around reading his book, or getting me to bend over the chart table in a suggestive manner, or opening another bottle of wine) and that the anchor chain was inclined to leap off its cog and plummet into the harbour like a manic lemming, no matter how careful I was, so that after a very short acquaintance with it I was starting to feel both incompetent and insecure.

"Ready with that anchor?" Roger would shout, standing by the wheel, looking important, and I would stand by, poised, in position, ready to go, then: disaster - I would press the button ("really gently and steadily, actually") and the anchor would leap cheerfully from its place and plunge into the depths taking its entire chain and the emergency rope with it.

"Aaaaarrrggggh! No! It's done it again! Bloody anchor!"
"Oh God, no! Holly! Can't you do anything properly?"
"I'm sorry, I can't seem to stop it -"
"Did you do it really gently and steadily, like I said?"
"Yes!"
"Oh dear."

There would now follow an interlude during which we fished the anchor out of the mud and then started all over again attempting to anchor. It was very stressful. Roger was an expert on stress, however.

"I think I need you to bend over the chart table again."
"Why?
"So that you can see where the next island is, and so that I can stand behind you and point to it over your shoulder. And I have some points of the compass to show you."
"Oh, OK. Mmmm."

One night, after a beautiful day's sailing, we anchored (amid the usual anchor crises) off an uninhabited island, to which we swam. There were sheep and the occasional ruined croft but otherwise, nothing but wildlife. It was beautiful. We saw a golden eagle, soaring like a guardian angel. After a thorough explore, Roger and I swam slowly back to the boat while the sunset unfolded itself in the sky like a red and gold banner. Back on the boat, to my surprise, Roger produced a joint.

"Where did you get that?"
"Never mind. Wow, Holly, look at that sky."

"I must warn you, I react really badly to cannabis, I get silly and then I fall asleep. Or if it's too strong it makes me sick. And than I go to sleep."

"Nonsense, it's just a bit disinhibiting."

I wondered if this was a good idea, given his medical condition, but I said nothing. We smoked in silence. I let him have most of it. The sunset deepened, quivered and gave way to stars of unaccustomed depth and shinyness. The universe expanded. It was warm, quiet, open; the scent of thyme and gorse on the slight breeze, the only sound that of the waves unlacing on the nearby shore. I lay back in Roger's (manly rope-sorry-yardheaving-type) arms and we watched shooting stars.

"Holly," Roger said.

"Yes, Roger?"

"I want a baby."

"I know."

"What do you think?"

"I think you would be a lovely dad."

"Shall we have a go at it?"

"What, me? I've got Nancy. I don't think I should do it again. Been there, done it, got the tee shirt etc."

"I'd like to have a baby with you."

"It's not a good plan. Ask Nancy. I'm a terrible mother."

"I think it is. I think it's an excellent plan."

"But -"

"Don't you want a boy? I want a boy."

"No, honestly, I -"

"You know what I want to do to you now? I want to take your clothes off and kiss you all over, and then I want to utterly impregnate you -"

"Do you? Oh, Roger!" - etc etc you can imagine what happened next.

The next morning I felt terrible, and not only because I was still stoned. I really really didn't want a baby but owing to my disinhibitedness I had gone and acted like I did want one. Oh what a hypocrite and pile of poo etc I was, my still malfunctioning brain nevertheless sternly informed me. I could only hope that my ageing body would laugh off this pitiful attempt at conception, and/or that I wasn't ovulating. I definitely wasn't in the mood for anchor wrestling, and luckily Roger was feeling even worse than I was, so we decided to stay put for the day.

It had turned out nice again, and so we decided (after a rather befuddled breakfast of coffee and stale doughnuts) to take the dinghy out for a spot of fishing. I put my bikini on, and Roger wore shorts and a Deep Purple tee shirt. We rowed to a nice sheltered spot which looked like a likely place for mackerel. Secretly I was hoping that we wouldn't catch anything because I knew who would have to gut the wretched things. However I wielded my spinner as if I was hoping to catch a whole flock, sorry, shoal of pesky mackerel.

We floated in silence. Not much happened. Some terns went past.

"Terns. Those were."
"Really?"
"Yes."
"Any particular kind of terns?"
"Almost certainly. Little, or arctic, or something."
"Well?"
"Dunno. Need the bird book."
"Oh."
Silence again.
"You know, Holly."
"What?"
"I really like you."
"I really like you too."
"Good."
"Yes."
"Hmm."
"Roger?"
"Mmmm?"

"There's a really big jellyfish over this side of the boat. I mean, massive."

"Really? Let's see. Wow, it is big. It's going right under the boat!"

"Yeah, wow."

"You get a lot of those big red ones at this time of year."

"Big."

"Yes. Nothing to worry about. Harmless. I'm fairly sure."

"Fuck!"

"What? Did you catch something?"

"No! Fuck!"

"What?"

"There's a fucking great jellyfish this side too!"

"No!"

"There fucking is! Look!"

"Fuck!"

"I know!"

"No, I mean, but fuck!"

"I said that!"

"Yes, but I mean, but fuck!"

"What the but fuck do you mean?"

"I mean, but fuck, it's the same fucking jellyfish as on my side!"

"Fuck no!"

"Yes! Look!"

"Oh, fuck!"

"It must be - what - seven - eight feet in diameter?"

"Fucking hell!"

We poked it with oars but it wasn't interested. We tried to row away from it but it was attached to us. We shouted at it. We hit it. It ignored us. I cried. Roger got cross with me. While we were thus employed, fat drops of rain began to fall. Suddenly, there was a flash of lightning, and almost immediately a huge crash of thunder, and it began to pour with rain. It brought us to attention. We started to row back to the boat as fast as we could, somewhat hampered by a giant jellyfish fastened to our underside. Roger was so cross, and so still stoned, that he began to row us round in circles.

"Fuck, where's the boat?"

"Over there, over there!"

"I can't make it!"

I took the oars from him and, pushing him aside, strenuously rowed towards the yacht, but the sea was getting up now with alarming speed and the waves started to hamper my view of where I was headed. Desperately, I kept rowing.

The yacht loomed up, and I tried to grab the rails so I could tie the dinghy to it. With a roar, Roger grabbed the rope (painter, as if I cared) from me and attempted to leap aboard. Unfortunately, as he was trying to bridge the gap between us and the boat, he slipped and fell into the sea.

"Roger!" I shrieked, jumping up. Now I had to deal with a drowning man, a giant jellyfish, an ever increasingly mountainous sea, and a rowing boat. I tired to grab Roger (hopeless, he was still stoned), I tried to pull him aboard as he was on the other end of the rope (hopeless, Roger was not paying enough attention), I tried to hit the jellyfish with an oar. I succeeded in losing an oar.

"No!" I shrieked. "The oar!"

Roger, who had appeared to be out of it, now came to and grabbed the oar as it floated past him. He passed it to me and attempted to clamber aboard.

"No! Get on the boat! Get on the boat! Not this boat! The other boat!"

"Let me in!"

"No! Get on the other boat!"

We had drifted near enough now for Roger to get onto the yacht. I poked him with the oar to make sure that he did.

"Catch the rope! The fucking rope!" Roger's reply was partly lost in the rising howl of the wind, but I got his drift.

"I don't care what it's fucking called! Just catch it!"

The rain was coming down in torrents now and we were both as wet as cats. I threw the rope. He didn't catch it.

"Oh my God!"

I threw it again, and this time Roger caught it, wavered on the edge of the boat, was about to fall in, then didn't, but dropped the rope again instead.

"You fucking idiot!"

"Well you throw like a fucking girl!"

"I am a fucking girl!"

"Well stop throwing like one!"

I threw it again. He caught it. He pulled. I was bobbing about like a tampon in a toilet as the waves became increasingly wild. I clambered aboard just as Roger let go of the rope and the boat bobbed off, looking pleased with itself but slightly panic-stricken like a child on a picnic escaping from its quarrelling parents.

"Bloody fuck!" Roger exploded, and raced to start the engine so that we could pursue the escapee.

"Can't we just leave it?"

"No we can not!"

"Alright!"

Now for about twenty minutes Roger raced around the dinghy, as the swell increased and the rain and wind strengthened, and I was supposed to catch the wretched thing with a hook on a stick.

"I don't care what the proper name for it is! I just don't care! Don't tell me the proper names for anything else!"

Roger looked a bit hurt but said nothing.

"For fuck's sake, Roger, can't you get any nearer? How long do you think my arms are? I'm not Stretch fucking Armstrong, you know!"

Roger muttered rude things about me under his breath and I shrieked swearwords at him but eventually I hooked the smug little boat and we headed for shelter to tie up. We lay at anchor, reading our respective books in separate cabins, for the rest of the day, while the wind howled around us. At supper time, I lurched into the tiny kitchen (sorry galley - as if I cared) to cook some pasta and tomato sauce. Above and beyond the call of duty I made meatballs incorporating wild thyme and mint from the island. Roger wolfed down his supper without comment, appreciative or otherwise.

We had a nice bottle of wine with the meal and after it Roger produced a bottle of whisky and started to knock it back. I washed up.

"Come on, Holly - you can't come to Scotland and not have some whisky. This is the real deal - a single malt so rare that you can only buy it at the distillery."

"Shouldn't you drink it a bit more slowly, in that case?"

"No. Not in these circumstances."

"Which circumstances?"

"Never mind."

"For goodness' sake."

"Just read your book. I'm going to listen to some music."

Roger put Leonard Cohen on very loud and began to drink harder than ever. I retreated to my cabin, but he came after me.

"And another thing," he shouted, "you tight bitch, what's with the fuckin' prancing about in a bikini all day and then playing little Miss Straight all night?"

"What is the problem, Roger?" I asked, trying to stay calm. I put my book down and sat upright. Roger was in the doorway, so there was no escape. Anyway, where would I go? Would I swim for a deserted shore in the dark, wind and rain?

"What's the problem? What's the fuckin' problem? She asks? Silly fuckin' bitch. I want to know what your fuckin' problem is? Why can't you be a bit more - you know what I'd like to do? What I'd really like to do? What really turns me on? Do you want to know?" His eyes were bloodshot and he seemed not to be really conscious of his surroundings. I started to be really rather scared. I really didn't want to know what really turned him on. Suddenly he backed away from the doorway and started to rummage in a kitchen drawer. I took my chance to get out of the tiny cabin and clamber hastily up the companion steps to the deck, where I gratefully breathed the ever-rising wind. I guessed Roger was looking for the corkscrew. I was wrong.

He appeared on deck a few moments later with the large kitchen knife in his hand. The one for cutting up large fish. This was the kind of body language that even I had no trouble deciphering.

"I know you're trying to make a fool of me," he said, in a calm manner which was much more frightening than if he had been shouting.

"Honestly, Roger, I'm not. I'm not doing anything of the kind," I burbled. Had he been missing his medication? Oh shit. I scampered forward towards the front of the boat (the bows - but who gives a fuck?) and prayed that my sober agility would defeat his determined but lurching intoxication.

"Come here, Holly. We need to talk."

His voice was kind of wheedling, creepy. I didn't want to antagonise him.

"I need a bit of space, Roger."

"Oh, I'll give you space."

There was a pause.

"Well, that's good. Isn't it. Because I need space and you're going to give me it. Lovely. So - er - what are you going to do now, Roger? Because -"

"I'm coming to find you, of course."

I could hear him coming, so I tried not to breathe noisily and crept round the deck in the opposite way. I could hardly see a thing, there was only a faint light escaping from the cabin and the boat was still bucketing about so it was difficult to move. Every rope I grabbed hold of appeared to be loose. It now occurred to me that Roger might fall overboard in his befuddled state and then I would lose one problem only to acquire a different one.

"Stop it, Roger," I shouted, sternly, over the ever-rising wind, trying to sound like his mother, "stop this silliness immediately, and go to bed!"

Of course, I had now given away my position and I heard a roar and a lot of shuffling - he was on the move again.

Clinging on to the rails for dear life I edged round towards the cabin, crouching low so that he wouldn't see me. Cautiously, I brought my head up so that I could see where I was - and looked straight into the eyes of Roger, who was creeping round the other way. We both stood up.

"Go to bed AT ONCE!" I shrieked.

"Yes - I'll go to bed now," he said meekly.

"Good. And let's not have any more of this nonsense, we've got a lot of sailing to do tomorrow. And give me that knife. Come on, hand it over."

"I don't want to."

"Give it to me, Roger, or I'll be very cross indeed."

He gave me the knife.

"Now off with you, and I don't want to hear a peep out of you until morning."

He went. I sat down and cried, then I hid the knife, and all the other knives, in my cabin, washed my face, and went to bed, locking my cabin door.

The next morning the sun was shining but there was still a stiff breeze and the sea was (to my eyes) bloody rough. Roger could only vaguely remember what had happened the night before, he apologised if he had upset me ("I sometimes get a bit down when I'm drunk") but as far as he was concerned, all was forgotten with the prospect of such a glorious day's sailing ahead of us. His eyes were bluer than ever as he scanned the horizon, joyously.

We set off after breakfast with the usual anchor shenanigans, and once out of our sheltered bay I realised that the waves were even higher than I had thought. The boat keeled over to an alarming extent and water sloshed over the side at regular intervals.

"Are we going to drown?" I shrieked.

"No, this is perfect sailing weather!"

"Oh God!"

It seemed I was not cut out for perfect sailing. I sat like a miserable wet kitten in my waterproof (put on rather too late) and held on tight as Roger, smiling ecstatically, drove the boat to harbour.

I have never been so happy to get on dry land. All the way I had been trying to remember some prayers (a vaguely C of E, liberal upbringing is very little use in a time of crisis, the only one I knew properly was the Lord's Prayer and even then I got muddled about trespasses). I had asked the Lord to make sure there was no fruit of our union, as I was quite certain that Rogerspawn would be way beyond my powers of motherhood to control. Mind you, I almost loved Roger again for having got me safely home.

"It's a terrible shame," Roger said suddenly, as we sat in a café, recovering, "but I have to go away for a week or two, on business, so this is the last time I'll see you for a while."

"That's a pity. Oh dear."

"Yes, I think we're getting on extraordinarily well," he said, "it's a shame to put the brakes on really."

Chapter 9

Snapdragon

Back home, I discovered that, as Basil has foretold, his ruse had been successful and we weren't going to court after all. I was faintly disappointed because I liked the idea of being in court with barristers and everyone swearing on bibles and a judge in a giant wig frowning as he heard the details of my dreadful ordeal and awarding me huge amounts of money. And donning a black cap and sentencing a certain person to death by hanging. That would be only right. Or maybe he would think I was a terrible wife and award everything to the other side. As it was, I got a massive cheque from Basil (minus his fees) and invited him out to dinner to celebrate.

"With your wife, of course," I added quickly, suspecting I could see Basil blushing.

"My wife doesn't socialise much," Basil said sadly, "but it was a kind thought."

"Oh well."

"So, this is the end of our association. I wish you every good outcome in the future. I'm sure a charming and beautiful young woman such as yourself will have a radiant future," Basil said, kissing me on the cheek. I cried. "And your daughter will sweep all before her." I cried even more. It was over. I was divorced, my new life was ahead of me, I had the money, I would never see Basil again. I kissed him back. He turned away, embarrassed, and we parted in that very clumsy English kind of way. For a moment I felt I was saying goodbye to the love of my life. Actually if he'd been a bit younger, and not married... no, no, ridiculous thought.

Nancy and I went out for a celebratory meal with Jane, who luckily arrived just as I could afford to accommodate her.

"The thing is, Holly, you've always just coasted along. If you'd had a proper career, you wouldn't be in this pickle now."

"I'm not in a pickle," I frowned, indicating Nancy with a movement of my head.

"Oh yes you are," Jane said. Her ability to read body language was clearly even worse than mine. And her a psychiatrist for heaven's sake. "You're in a terrible pickle. Where are you going to live? You can't stay in this godforsaken place -"

Nancy and I both sat up, indignantly straight.

"- you'll have to move down south to be nearer the rest of us. You can get a proper job, and we can find a good school for Nancy to go to for her A levels."

"I like the school I'm at now, Aunty Jane," Nancy said. Her words were polite but her tone was arctic. "I like my friends and I'm very happy." Jane took no notice whatever.

"I know mum would like you to be nearer home, you could be really useful to her with shopping and things, I'd like to do more but I just don't have time with the boys and the job and so on. Now, you'd be in a perfect position, because Nancy's nearly grown up now and doesn't really need you any more."

Nancy and I looked at each other speechless for a moment and then, both seeing the funny side at once burst out laughing. Nancy fell into my arms.

"I can't manage without her - I have special needs," she cackled.

Jane looked very disapproving, as unfortunately she is a psychiatrist specialising in aberrant adolescent behaviour, but she said nothing, turning her attention back to her scallops Florentine. I thought I could see the greedy gene, so prominent in dear Nancy, at work in another member of the family. Why didn't either of them get fat? So unfair.

"I don't think you realise that I actually like living here."

"What rubbish - you only moved to Yorkshire because that man dragged you up here!" Jane replied a little too loudly, causing other diners to look up from their tasteful plates of seafood.

"I grew up here - we grew up here, in case you have forgotten! Have you excised this part of your past from the official history?"

"You need to buy a house somewhere! You can't possibly want to stay in Yorkshire! It's the perfect time to move." "I'm going to stay in the rented flat for now, while Nancy is still at school. It's decided."

"You can't rent! It's money down the drain!"

"I'll buy something as well."

"Where?"

"I'm thinking about France."

Jane snorted.

"I might have known you'd have some half-baked idea like that."

"I'm making plans to go over there and study the market."

"Oh you've got it all worked out then, so you don't need me," Jane said huffily, tucking into her main course, which had just arrived, of pan-fried turbot with wild mushrooms, wilted dandelion leaves and pink peppercorns. Or something.

"It's very nice to see you, anyway."

"Huh."

"Is mum alright?"

"She thinks she is - but I don't think she's coping very well. Last time I went round, there was a dead mouse in the kitchen and mum hadn't even noticed. She thought it was a shrivelled mouldy carrot. She said she couldn't bend over to pick it up, because of her back. I'm worried about her, actually. And there's you living in this bloody awful dump when you could be helping her..."

"Nancy - school - did I not explain properly?"

"She can transfer, like I said."

"I don't want to," Nancy interrupted.

"Children don't always know what's in their best interests," Jane said in a trying earnestly not to sound patronising but failing voice.

"I'm glad you're not my psychiatrist," said Nancy, viciously. Jane took no notice.

"And anyway it's not a dump. Have you actually looked around you? Here you are, eating a delicious meal for half the price you'd pay in Hadley-on-Thames, people are polite and don't try to rip you off all the time, well, only some of them do, the schools are fantastic and children actually want to learn something, there are real hills instead of those poxy Hillterns, there's no hosepipe ban - why do you need to tell yourself it's so much better down south?" I added.

"Because it is. The weather is better, for a start."

"The weather's better in Waikiki, so why not go there?"

"So you aren't going to look after your mother in her time of crisis?"

"No, I'm going to look after my daughter in her time of crisis."

"I see."

"And last time I saw mum she seemed to be absolutely fine. I really don't see how she can be struggling if she's still getting away for five holidays a year."

"Can we go now, mum?" Nancy said in a tone of voice which I recognised as dangerous.

"Bill, please!" I exclaimed as a waiter passed.

"But what about pudding?" Jane said.

We got home, but only just. At several points, Nancy threatened to walk off into the night. In the end I blackmailed her by reminding her that the next day was my birthday. We all went to bed in a sulk, after I had unfolded the sofa bed in a sulk and made it up for Jane in a sulk.

My birthday dawned; an unusually bright day, as if trying to prove to Jane that this north/south stuff was just rubbish. Not only that, but the weather forecast got in on the act, predicting cold, rainy and even stormy conditions in the south east. Jane tried to hide her rage, but later rang her husband ("to check on the children") and I overheard her ask him about the weather. He must have replied in kind, because her next remark was:

"Well, surprisingly warm. But the flowers aren't so far advanced."

So that was alright then. The bell rang while we were eating breakfast (fantastic freshly baked bread from our local bakery and local bacon from our wonderful butcher, I hoped Jane would notice) and I went to the door to be greeted by a florist with the most beautiful roses I had ever seen deep crimson and scented like a whole summer garden.

"Ooh," Jane said, "he's quite keen, isn't he?"

"Hmm," I said.

Nancy slipped a parcel across the table. It was book sized, and in a brown paper bag tied round with red hair ribbon.

"Happy Birthday, mum."

It was Roger's Profanisaurus.

"What's that?" asked Jane, who had never heard of it.

"Book - comedy," I said, hastily hiding it.

"I thought you could keep it by the loo," said Nancy with an air of innocence which did not match the coughing fit which came upon her as she tried not to laugh.

"Those croissants are far too rich," said Jane, crossly, thumping Nancy on the back.

"Now she's choking. Get a glass of water."

I didn't. When Nancy stopped, Jane gave me her present.

"It's from mum, too. We clubbed together."

It was a watercolour of Hadley-on-Thames. "By a wonderful local artist, and a lovely girl, mum says, mum got to know her at her bridge club, she's really good and we wanted to encourage her, and remind you of how beautiful home is."

"But it's not home," I said, quite annoyed now, especially at the thought of the money wasted on this meritless daub. "It's just somewhere you decided to live."

"Where we put down roots, Holly."

"Well, I put down roots here."

"Nonsense."

"How dare you say nonsense like that? I love it here!"

"We love it here," Nancy added, icily.

"There you go." I said.

"I see. It seems it won't be possible to help you then, as you've already made your mind up. Mother will be disappointed."

"She won't. She'll be gadding off to Burkina Faso or somewhere. Is it remote and does it have a romantic name? She'll get there, try and stop her."

"I do try and stop her. She's not up to all this travelling, and you just seem to encourage her. It's killing her."

"Maybe it's the way she wants to go. With a smile on her lips as she lies under the stars by a campfire surrounded by ululating tribesmen."

"You're so irresponsible."

"I'm not. I think she's an adult and she can make her own decisions. Like me, in fact. Actually."

"I can see there's no point in talking to you about this."

"Good."

I had arranged for Carla to come over for drinks in the evening, and a couple of old friends from the village had promised to make the great trek out of the dale too, so it would almost be a party. I'd asked Anders and his wife as well, but they couldn't come. Roger was still away. (Fortunately). Nancy now excused herself, and said she would be staying with a friend overnight. I could see she was upset by Jane, so I didn't ask many questions. It wasn't always safe to push Nancy when she was upset.

"Shall I drop you off?"

"Oh, it's ok, I'll get the bus."

"What, now?"

"Yes."

"I'll see you to the door then."

"Why the Profanisaurus, dear daughter?" I hissed as I pretended to see her to the door.

"You've got to get over all this romantic flowers and babies stuff, mother, it's not real. Read what men really think about women."

"Honestly darling, I think I know a bit more about men than you do."

"I should hope so, but I think you need to know more about the dark side. You're such a sweet, innocent mother," she added as she tucked her hair into a beret. "I don't want you to get hurt."

And with that, she left, slamming the door hard to let Jane know that she was not forgiven.

I was hoping she didn't know what I knew of the dark side. The party was terrible. It was an anti-party. Jane was wearing a black dress which was the opposite of an LBV, being long and linen and flowing, the kind of dress a hippy widow would wear. My friends from the village, Ian and Maggie, spent the evening moaning about how boring the village was these days, not because I had left, which would have been gratifying to hear, but because too many houses were being bought as holiday cottages.

"It's not the same. It's just dead in the winter," Maggie complained, "no-one goes in the pub any more because the landlord's been awful ever since his wife ran away with another woman -"

"No-one told me this?"

"It was about when you were having your problems too, I suppose I couldn't get a word in edgewise."

I was a little hurt by this remark.

"She met her on the internet, apparently. There's all sorts on there. Have you tried internet dating?"

"Not yet. Er - and how are the children?" I topped up her gin and tonic, but it was in vain.

"Oh don't get me started! You know Millie failed her eleven plus? And then we spent all that time appealing? Well, now we can't get her in to the private school we chose, we have to have a rethink, and we're running out of time -"

Meanwhile Carla, who had on a low-cut top, was getting on very well indeed with Ian, and Maggie, who was a lovely person, usually, but a bit inclined to wear padded waistcoats and trackie bottoms, kept shooting her hostile glances. As I could have predicted, at nine-thirty she announced that the babysitter had to be home early so they would have to go. They went. Which left me, Jane and Carla.

"Pass me that bottle," said Carla, "I think it's still got some wine in it."

"Certainly," said Jane, passing it.

"Are you not having some more to drink, Jane?" Carla enquired.

"I think I've had enough," she said with emphasis. Her long silver earrings bobbed disapprovingly.

"I think you haven't," giggled Carla. "You should loosen up a bit, you know, it is healthy for you."

"What about coffee?" Jane enquired pointedly.

I'm sure she expected me to go and make it for her, but I didn't. I was sick of being bossed about. I hunted in vain for another open bottle with some remaining contents, and when I failed to find one, I opened a new one. Jane gave me a look which I was happy to be unable to interpret, as she went into the kitchen to put the kettle on.

"I have heard some interesting news about my former husband," Carla began when we were alone. "He wants to settle the case, my solicitor says. Things are moving at last!"

"That's great! What's the next step?"

"I have to raise some money for the court - but I will get it back of course."

"I can lend you some now," I exclaimed, "I've got my settlement! How much do you need?"

"No, that's not possible because it would be maybe as much as ten thousand pounds."

"I've got that much!"

"No. Not possible. I would not even hear of it."

"But I'd like to help -"

"Help with what?" asked Jane, coming back into the sitting room with her coffee.

"I have all kinds of projects," Carla said, throwing a dazzling smile at Jane, "my life is insanely complicated! I'm sure yours is too?"

"I juggle so many things I don't get much time for projects. If I get half and hour a week to myself to read a book it's a miracle. I have three young sons and a very demanding job."

"What is it that you do?"

"I'm a psychiatrist."

"Oh," said Carla.

"Most people don't know what to say. Usually because they have something they think they need to keep hidden"

"It must be - very interesting."

"Sadly, no. Most mad people are very boring."

"Oh." There was a short silence.

"Tell Carla about the man who thought the bus driver was God."

"Oh, he doesn't think that any more. Not since, according to him, God dropped him off at the wrong stop."

"Nancy would think that was a metaphor."

"I'm more interested in people who try to deceive other people than in people who try to deceive themselves, just now," Jane said, sipping her coffee.

"Oh, have you got some good ones?" I asked eagerly. Sometimes Jane could be chatty and interesting about her cases.

"I can't talk about individuals," she sniffed. "I'm a professional."

There was another small silence. Carla got off the sofa and started to look for her coat.

"Are you going, Carla?"

"Yes, I have to go. I hope to see you very soon, my dear Holly."

"I just opened another bottle?"

"I had forgotten, I have said I will go in early tomorrow to catch the Italian businessmen when they are at their most vulnerable and tell them about - what is it this week? Mobile phone contracts. With the hour difference that means seven in the morning! I will see you there?"

"No, I have a contract in the accounts department - it's dreadfully dull. Catch you at lunchtime, though."

"Goodnight, dearest Holly," said Carla, kissing me on both cheeks, twice, "I will be seeing you soon." And she vanished into the night.

"She seems nice," Jane said. "Bright. Interesting."

"Oh she is, I really like her, and she's been so supportive."

"I'm glad you have some friends. It's very nice for you. But you mustn't be too selfish. If only you could be closer to your family -"

"Just shut up!" I shouted. (It was the wine shouting.) "I've had enough of this! I don't care about the bloody family! I'm only bothered about Nancy! Now get out of my hair!"

"There's no need to shout."

"Sometimes there is!"

"I think I'll get ready for bed now."

"Yes - you do that - and I'll get off the sofa so you can do that - and the duvet's here, and the sheet's under that chair, shall I get it, and I'm going to bed too and I won't be here in the morning!" I wasn't exactly shouting, but I was a bit loud.

"I'll clean the place for you tomorrow."

"Oh. That would be nice of you." I calmed down. Gosh, Jane was nice! And I was so horrible, and drunk, probably. I really didn't deserve her. I apologised for shouting, and I went to bed in a haze of confused happiness, everyone was so lovely. As Basil had said, everything was going to be just fine. I had been firm with my family, flexible with my daughter and helpful to my friend, and now I was going to reap the reward for my goodness.

Chapter 10

I'm too depressed to think of a title for chapter ten.

I got the paper from the supermarket on Saturday evening after I dropped Jane off at the station. I was sitting in the car and got the listings section out to check what was on at the cinema, so I could take Nancy to see something. We were both rather big animation fans. Idly, I turned the pages and ran my eye down the lonely hearts section.

"Passionate, forty-something seafarer seeks younger mermaid for happy family times."

Why did I immediately think that this was Roger? It could be Roger. It sounded exactly like the kind of advert Roger would write. Ooh. We hadn't exactly split up, either.

"Mermaid? What the hell's he want a fucking mermaid for?" I exploded all over Nancy when I got home.

"Aah, sweet little merbabies, how gorgeous. I can see them now - a perfect little family of Sea Monkeys -"

"You are NO help at all. Horrible daughter."

"I don't want to help. I want you to move right on, mother, now. Snap out of this spineless gibbering. Relationships, bollocks! Everyone gets what they want to get out of it. Some people want money, some want babies and some want security. There are a million reasons for hooking up with someone. Only sad bastards like you believe in true love."

"I did love him, you know. For a while."

"I know - it always seems like that at the time."

"I sort of thought we might work things out..."

But even Nancy, who didn't know what had happened in Scotland, could tell that this was delusional.

"You were going to grow a fishy tail and turn into his mermaid? Bless your heart."

"How did you get so cynical?"

"Er - der - I had you and dad for parents. Now, take this cup of tea, and make a list of what you really want to do with your life, and read it to me. Tomorrow."

Actually, I did as I was told. And the next morning, I was ready.

"Well?" She was half way through a fresh loaf and the bilberry jam was on its last scraping. She was leaning against the washing machine, in which her hardware store uniform was revolving gently.

"I've got my list."

"Read it."

"First of all, most importantly, I want to bring you up and get you into university, or whatever you decide to do. So I want to stay here until you're eighteen."

"What about the French thing?"

"That's next on the list. I want to buy a house in France and do it up so that I can run courses there. Birdwatching, photography, poetry, that kind of thing. But I want to spend a few years setting it up, by which time you'll be eighteen."

"Good plan."

"I thought so. You could help me in the holidays."

"What else?"

"I want to grow an apricot tree."
"That's good. Anything else?"
"I want to see an albatross."
"Excellent. And?"
"Learn to appreciate abstract art."
"OK. Is there much more?"
"That's just the start of the As."
"Aha. I was beginning to suspect. Is it an exhaustive list?"
"It exhausted me. I was up till three."
"That'll have to do for now. You can tell me the rest later. I have to get to work. I can't be here all morning. Just tell me - does the Sea Monkey feature in this plan? At all?"
"Nope."
"Good."

I folded up the rest of my list and tucked it into my pocket. It had been a good thing to do. I had realised just how full and rich and curranty the world was, and how little of it I knew.

Dear reader, please feel free to write your own list here, and to continue on the flyleaf if you run out of room. I always used to draw on the flyleaves (flyleafs?) of my books when I was a child and I still think of it as legitimate space for creative endeavour.

Roger rang me up at teatime. Nancy and I had been bilberry picking, and were seriously purple, all over.

"It'll never come out," Nancy was wailing in the background by the sink as she scrubbed with a nailbrush at the tyrian arse of her favourite pair of jeans.

"Hi, Holly, is it a good time?"
"As good as any."

"Who is it? It's him, isn't it?" Nancy remarked, offstage.

"I was hoping to meet up with you soon. I can't wait to see you again. I brought you a present from Mexico. You'll love it."

"Oh, how nice."

"The bastard."

"You sound - er - different. Is someone there?"

"Only Nancy."

"Has something happened?"

"I don't know Roger. Has something happened? You tell me. I can't imagine what kind of response you've had to your advert."

There was a short silence.

"Oh. That. Did you see it?"

"Yes."

"I'm sorry. The thing is -"

"Bye, Roger. Good luck with the sealife."

"Bye Roger! Well done, mother," Nancy said, jumping around and kissing me effusively.

"What a star. And you didn't lose your cool. Well done. Way to go!"

"I'm a bit sad though," I said, kissing her in return but turning away so she wouldn't see my face. "Even though he was horrid."

I didn't want her to know how unhappy I was. I went to my room and sobbed silently for about an hour. Then it seemed to be over, for now. There. My first foray into true love, after divorce. And it ended in tears, of course. Damn. One of the things I learnt from this episode was that, when you are newly divorced, your children can be wiser and more understanding of the truth than you are. In some ways they become your parent. If they give you advice, it is a good idea to pay attention, because they could be seeing something you, in your golden mist of illusion, have failed to spot. It could be a massive rock looming up on your starboard bow.

So, of course, I didn't think things could get much worse (unless, of course, I was pregnant), and I went relatively cheerfully to the accounts (and supplies) department of the call centre where I was to work as a temp the next day, thinking that at least it would be a distraction from the despair that otherwise loomed over my life like a slow-moving cold weather system from the Atlantic. I was shown up to the very top of the building, where Suzanne, John and Harvey, between them, made sure that everything ran smoothly in the world of call centre finance.

"You sit here," Suzanne said, "then Harvey can look up your skirt." She and John burst into maniacal laughter at this, while Harvey looked as if he might cry.

"OK," I said cautiously. "What shall I do?"

"Well," John said, "you turn the computer on with this button here," and he and Suzanne became hysterical again, and Harvey slowly opened a packet of mints, while staring out of the window at a tree.

I could see that it was going to be a long day, and indeed, for the first time since I left school, I spent the day glancing at the clock every five minutes hoping that it was later than I thought. It didn't seem possible that I could sink any lower. Suzanne and John evidently had some kind of relationship, and I was guessing that, not long ago, Harvey had had a similar relationship with Suzanne, or possibly with John. Suzanne kept teasing Harvey with scarcely veiled sexual references.

"Oooh, I'm so hot, I'm perspiring, I'm positively wet," she giggled, while John bent double in his swivel chair, snorting with laughter, and Harvey sat rigid, typing numbers frantically with his right hand while he held a phone with his left. I couldn't quite work out what it was that made Suzanne so desirable, she was at least as old as I was, possibly older, she wore sensible twinsets and skirts and high heeled court shoes, her hair was short and tidy and she appeared to me to have all the sex appeal of the Queen. On the other hand, John and Harvey were exceptionally dull and unattractive and so, presumably, in their world Suzanne represented an almost unattainable ideal of femininity and sexiness.

"I'm so glad to have got that off my chest! What's that man called again? Nicholas? Knickerlarse? Knicker elastic? Ha ha ha ha ha -" and she was off again. Also I gathered, from her endless remarks about herself, that she was seriously keen on housework, a quality which I imagined many a bachelor would find alluring, just as many a spinster would be turned on by a man who was good at DIY, fantasising about all those little jobs being done. Maybe bachelors fantasise about people keeping the loo clean and baking scones?

By the end of the week I was so crazed by boredom and the horror of listening to Suzanne laughing at things that simply weren't funny - "Oh, John, guess what, I got some bunny bedsocks! I know!" she would shriek - and the gloom and angst of Harvey, on the phone telling people that if they didn't settle their accounts in ten days he would send Suzanne round to drive them insane (that's what I would have done, I bet the customers could hear her cackling in the background, the old witch) that I was almost prepared to go without a week's pay rather than put myself through it again, but Nancy told me on Friday night that she needed fifty pounds to go on a camping holiday with her friends, and that if I could lend it to her...

Lending, in Nancy-speak, is not the same as lending in the normal sense. She never feels bad about it, but nor does she ever pay it back. So I went back to accounts on Monday, in the deepest darkest despair. I sat at the desk, processing orders on the computer and then transferring paper copies of the same orders from one box to another, and then recording the fact that I had done so in another programme on the computer in a kind of parody of efficiency. It was as if I had wandered into a Swiftian satire, a Kafkaesque bureaucracy which existed only in order to perpetuate itself. However, after half an hour or so, I started to pay attention to my surroundings instead of wallowing in literary parallels and I noticed something strange. No-one was talking. No-one was laughing, either, in fact, a strange and slightly strained peace reigned in finance. Something had happened. What was it?

"Holly," said an over-polite voice to my left, "could you pass me a paperclip please?"

Suzanne had a dishful of paperclips on her desk, and I was about to point this out, when I realised that overtures were being made, and in the interests of having a bearable week at work, I decided to co-operate.

"Here you are, Suzanne. Have a few while we're at it. Take a handful. Nice weekend?"

"Oh, so-so. Actually, not really. I got all my kitchen cupboards sorted out though, that was one blessing." She sighed deeply.

"Oh dear. I mean, good about the cupboards."

"Did you have a nice weekend, Holly?"

"I think I slept through most of it."

"It is very tiring working here. People don't appreciate how stressful this job is."

"Well let me assure you that I do."

"Thanks, Holly. It's nice to be appreciated for what you do. Most people just don't realise. Well, not many people make it up this far in the building, do they, it's only us godlike beings live up this high isn't it?"

She kept glancing at John, but John was deep in problem accounts and never looked over once. Occasionally, his hairy ears quivered with emotion, but clearly there was a rift between John and Suzanne.

Then I noticed something else. Harvey had gone.

"Where's Harvey?" I asked.

"Off sick. I don't actually think there's anything the matter with him, but he rang up saying he had a sore throat and a temperature. I hope he doesn't expect me to go and mop his brow! We have a temp coming in, god help us, no offence Holly, but temps! Honestly! Temps of doom I call them, don't I, John?"

But Suzanne was snorting with laughter alone. Towards lunchtime the silence of accounts was broken by the sound of someone clattering up the stairs and the door opened to reveal Henk, the grumpy Dutchman. I couldn't say I was delighted to see him, but at least he was a familiar face and he might actually break the silence occasionally.

"Hello Henk!"

"Do you know each other then?"

"Yes, we worked together on a project. It was not a great success, I believe," Henk said. "Where do I sit?"

"You can be here, next to me," Suzanne said, turning the full force of her attention on Henk, who sank promptly and obediently into the chair by her side, almost trapping her patting hand beneath his generous buttocks as he did so. I began to see how Suzanne did it.

"Soooooo, Henk, is it, whereabouts are you from, that's a lovely accent, makes me feel all goose pimply," Suzanne cooed, undoing the top few buttons of her cardigan as she spoke. I started to feel a bit ill, and I suspect John did too.

"I am Dutch," Henk said, not even scowling.

"Golly, Dutch, how cosmopolitan! John went to Amsterdam once, didn't you John?" John would have preferred to ignore this, as the trembling of his ears indicated, but he turned graciously and said:

"Welcome to accounts, Hank, or whatever your name is. I'm sorry, but I'm very busy and I can't make conversation today, polite or otherwise. I do hope you'll all excuse me," and with that he turned his back once more and resumed the feverish five finger exercises with his right hand that made Ashkenazy look like a butterfingered clod. Suzanne and Henk found an excuse to go to the far side of the room shortly after that (so that Suzanne could show Henk the correct procedures, apparently) and apart from their muffled sniggering it was quiet again.

At lunch I asked Henk, who was eating a large fried egg bap at his desk, how the tower of Babel (as I liked to think of it) was getting on without me. Suzanne had gone to get a diet coke from the machine, and left him alone for five minutes.

"They have found very good native speaker, he is a student I think, Martine's nephew, Jean-Claude," - Ha! Treachery, I might have known - "and they have yet to find replacement for Carla."

"Is Carla leaving?"

"Didn't you know? She went. No-one know where she is." He

picked his teeth with his fingernail and wiped something on his jumper.

"But I only saw her last week - at lunchtime on Tuesday -"

"She didn't come in on Thursday, no warning, nothing. Martine was very very pissed. Then Friday, Carla don't come in again, Martine is hitting the ceiling, she is so pissed."

"Gosh what a mental picture. Sounds like Martine. But what do you mean, no-one knows where Carla is?"

"She doesn't answer her phone, or her mobile, and when Anders goes to her home on Friday night, she is not there. No-one is there."

"Did she go on holiday? Or maybe she went abroad to sort out her divorce? Her mobile phone might not work? There could be lots of reasons."

Henk shrugged. How was it that Europeans thought that a shrug was an actual reply? How annoying.

"Don't you know anything else about Carla? Don't you care?" I demanded. Henk just looked at me like the hapless piece of blubber he was.

"You're getting on terribly well with Suzanne," I said nastily. I was cross now. His colleague vanishes, and he doesn't give a toss. He would feel the same about me. And to think I had been pleased to see him.

Henk blushed, and fiddled with his watch.

"I don't suppose you know how old she is?" I was in a very unpleasant mood, for which I blamed the accounts department. It was twisting my mind.

"She's your age - or a bit older, I'm not entirely sure how old you are." I was about to enlighten him when he said:

"She's thirty-five. Biological clock, ha, ha," and started to eat a chocolate mousse, getting chocolate all round his mouth like a large toddler. I couldn't watch, so I galloped down four flights to talk to Martine, who might be treacherous, but at least had table manners.

"Martine - Henk just told me about Carla!"

"I don't know anysing, why should I know? All I know is I have to find another Italian speaker, vite vite! I am very annoyed with

Carla. I don't actually care what happened to her, she is very unprofessional, but if you care, Anders might know somesing." Martine was in one of her Frenchest moods, so I tentatively approached Anders, who still made me feel a bit funny. I had been avoiding him on account of the funny feelings. He had a particularly fetching blue shirt on today, with the sleeves rolled up, and was kind of clean and outdoor fresh, like a sunny conifer forest. I expect his wife had taken extra care with the ironing.

"Hello, Anders, how's it going?"

"It goes well, Holly, and how about your life?"

"Splendid and excellent, Anders," (I never knew what I was saying to Anders, words just made themselves up) "my daughter just finished her exams and I just dumped my boyfriend, you know, that sort of thing, oh, and my divorce came through."

"Really? Are you pleased?"

"Relieved. Hey, what can I say?"

What could I say, I was on automatic pilot, I just had to pray that my settings were accurate as I no longer had control over what words came out of my mouth.

"We should go for a drink, to celebrate."

"Gosh, that would be lovely." (Did I say that? Help.)

"What about Thursday?"

"Thursday would be fab, Anders, I look forward to it, this is my phone number -" (no! no!) "- tell me when and where. See you." And I fled back upstairs in a panic, to review what had just happened. I had made a date with a married man on whom I had (I was forced to admit) a bit of a crush. Hence the funny feelings. I was incapable of using my brain in his presence. I had recently had a crushing blow in the love department. What was I thinking of?

Back upstairs, Henk and Suzanne were in the stock cupboard (as she came out very briefly to tell me, she was showing him what was what, and where it went) while John was out at the pub for lunch. I did as little as possible (clock watching all afternoon) and rushed home as soon as I could, gagging to tell Nancy about the days events. There was no Nancy. I rang her mobile.

"I'm working, mum, remember?" she said when she answered at last. (I kept redialling until she did). "Babysitting?"

"Oh yes, but you didn't say today."

"Yes I did, mum, I don't think you can have been listening. Maybe you had too much to drink the night before -"

"Enough cheek!"

"Anyway, that's where I am."

"Where exactly? What's the number?"

"Oh," she said vaguely, "I've got my mobile, not sure what the landline is."

"Address?"

"Something Drive, I forget, somewhere in Morton Spa anyway. Do you want me to ask? They're still here, on their way out. They've got the sweetest little baby. Called Felicity."

"Aaaah, how sweet," I said briefly, then, "do you need a lift home?"

"No, I'll get a lift back."

"See you later then. Er - what sort of time?"

"They don't know, it's a party, they're going to leave before two anyway."

"Two? In the morning?"

"It's alright, mum, no school, remember."

"Hmmm."

I particularly wasn't happy that I had no-one to talk to about the mystery of the disappearing Italian friend, so in desperation I rang Jane.

"I don't know what you're making such a fuss about! Honestly Holly, you always exaggerate!"

"I'm worried that something has happened to her!"

"Nothing has happened to her! Honestly! Anyway, she's an adult!"

"So, how are the boys, then?"

"Oh God, don't talk about it, Dougie has an entrance exam next week!"

"I thought you were firmly opposed to private education?"

"It's a comprehensive, allegedly, well, it's the best one round here anyway. It's so popular they do this gruesome test. Dougie's getting coaching for it."

"I see."

"There's no need to be so smug!"

"I'm not being smug, really. It's just that we do have such excellent schools in the North..."

"Well, we have some lovely ones too, it's just that - "

"They're the private ones?"

"Anyway, let's not talk about that. What did you ring for again?"

"That Italian friend of mine, you met?"

"You know an Italian?"

"You met her."

"Oh, for heaven's sake, I thought you meant a man."

"Well, she's disappeared."

"Oh, I see. Yes, but Holly, it's not your problem, is it."

"She's my friend."

"You have enough real problems, Holly," Jane said firmly, "without inventing new ones. How's that niece of mine? I was a bit worried about her when I saw her."

"But Jane, how could you worry about Nancy? She's just fine!"

Chapter 11

Butler in the Pantry

My date with Anders was such a cause of stress to me that I nearly didn't go at all, but in the end I decided that it was in the interests of finding Carla, so I went. We met in a pub in Milltown, I was fairly certain that it was one I had been to with Carla but I couldn't be sure. I was keeping my eyes peeled, though, for the man in the brown jacket. Bearing in mind that he might occasionally wear something else.

I was there a bit early and so witnessed the entrance of Anders, whereupon the eyes of every woman in the room swivelled automatically in his direction. That man should have been doing adverts for washing powder, as he was surrounded by an aura of freshly laundered fresh launderedness which was clearly some kind of major aphrodisiac for women of all ages. Honestly, his poor wife. She must have spent ages maintaining that crisp dry aura. Thus I was the object of focussed hatred and envy as he strode to my table and pecked me on the cheek.

"Hello, Holly, how are you doing?"

"Just great, thanks, got a new car," I burbled.

"What kind you get?"

"A Volvo."

"Ah, Swedish car," said Anders with great satisfaction. "The best cars."

"Do you have a Swedish car?"

"I have a Peugeot."

"Oh, OK."

He went to get himself a drink, and, as I watched him make his way to the bar, followed by the gaze of every woman in the room, I wondered if anyone else knew Carla here. When Anders came back, I said,

"I've decided I'm going to ask the man at the bar about Carla."

"I'll come with you."

So we both pulled up bar stools and I got the attention of the barman. He was a gloomy man with pink cheeks and boiled eyes. It was a quiet evening.

"Just you on then?"

"'Aving to do t'lot, aye. As per bloody usual."

"Including chatting to the customers?"

"If I must."

"Are you here often?"

"Does yer boyfriend mind you chattin' me up?"

"He's a work colleague," I laughed artificially. "What's your name, anyway?"

"Mick," said Mick, as reluctantly as it is possible to utter one syllable.

"Are you here most nights?"

"I'm here every soddin night," Mick said bitterly, "and taxi all day, worn to a string, I am, payin' off t' kitchen, and t' double glazing, and t' new carpets, and now it's only a new bathroom suite she wants next. An' yer know, when I took 'er in, she were a single mother, not everyone would ave ad er, damaged goods an all that," he added confidingly. "I did expect 'er to be a bit more grateful. But as soon as we were wed, the mood changed dramatically."

"Do you have any crisps?" I asked to change the subject.

"Mustard and japanese onion, tarragon vinegar and garlic, or organic horseradish," he recited glumly.

"Ugh. Do you have any normal crisps?"

"No." He looked at me sadly. "Brewery policy. Tek t'place upmarket."

"Mmmm. Speaking of upmarket," I continued, casually, "do you know a glamorous Italian woman who comes in here regularly?"

He looked anxious, for a few seconds, then he looked as if he was thinking hard.

"I don't think so - ? No, don't ring a bell at all."

"Short, dark, skinny, big boobs, enormous earrings?"

"Nope. No-one like that. I'd remember, wouldn't I?" Now he looked absolutely confident, if I was any judge.

"Recommended this pub to us, didn't she, Anders? Sure it was this one? Said is was upmarket. Maybe we got the wrong one. Maybe we should write and ask the brewery -?"

"Oh, her."

"Yes. Her."

"Big dry white wine drinker?"

"The very same. Have you seen her recently?"

"Ooh, let me think, when did I last see Carla? Hoi!" he shouted across the bar, "when was the last time Carla were in 'ere? Were it last week?"

The man addressed as Hoi approached. I looked at him closely. It was possible that he was the man in the brown jacket, now wearing a beige linen number with the sleeves rolled up over a green tee shirt in retro Miami Vice style.

"Not seen her. Anyway, I don't really know her. What did you say her name was?"

"I didn't," I said.

"Think we had a chat, once," Miami Vice, or Hoi went on. "she were telling me she had this friend who was divorced and a bit desperate, if you know what I mean."

"You mean she tried to set us up?"

"Were that you? I don't think that's right. She said she were dead good-looking - think she must 'ave meant another friend, love, no offence. Anyroad - sorry pal" (that was to Anders) "- can't waste any more valuable supping time."

And so saying he moved decisively away.

"I am not even slightly convinced by this rigmarole!" I exclaimed.

"When opening hours have been extended, as everyone knows," said Anders.

"Saying that Carla was trying to set him up with me! As if! I'm sure he's the man I've seen before, I recognise the patchy stubble. And he was pretending he didn't know her name - I never said her name. The barman knew it, too. And he pretended he didn't know her at first, too. I'm very worried for her, Anders. Something funny is going on here."

"I think you should stop concerning yourself, Holly. Carla is a big girl -"

"She's tiny!" I interrupted.

"An old girl then. What in Swedish we call a she-wolf with many suns in her eyes."

"I see. Is that complimentary or insulting? In Swedish?"

Anders shrugged, and his shoulders went up and down with his shirt in a way that made me forget all about Carla, and wolves, and shifty barmen, indeed anything at all for a bit. Somehow, Anders' continental shrugs were not at all like Henk's. After a very pleasant evening, during the course of which I had an entirely satisfactory snog in the car with Anders, the married tart, I made my way home in a confused emotional state. Should I be worried about Carla? Well, I was worried, anyway. I didn't trust Hoi Miami Vice - damn, never found out his name - I didn't trust the barman, and Anders' wife definitely shouldn't trust Anders.

I drove slowly home with a lot of different things swimming around my conscious mind like hyperactive koi carp in an inadequately sized pond. I felt quite exhausted when I pulled onto the drive and let myself into the hall.

I was revived instantly when Nancy told me she had taken a call from Goodfun Productions in my absence, they had a hole in their schedule because someone had pulled out at the last minute, and could we go to France in ten days?

"I can do it, but what about you, Nance?"

"Alright."

I was so excited that I ignored the fact that she seemed a bit vague and listless.

"Why are they ringing in the evening?"

"How would I know? It was Helena, she's going to be our researcher. She'll ring again tomorrow to find out exactly what you want."

Nancy took herself off to bed to avoid further excited and unanswerable questions from me, so I did the same. Naturally I couldn't sleep, and when I did, I had the very strangest dreams in which we found Carla bound and gagged in the cellars of an empty chateau, and Anders drove us all home in a giant Swedish van.

"I bet it means you're a closet lesbian," said Nancy unhelpfully when I recounted my vivid dream over breakfast. "Finding women in your cellar? Think about it. It's pretty obvious to me. That'll be why you're so obsessed with finding her, you're in love, but you won't admit it."

"Oh, bog off to work, horrible daughter," I said, because Nancy was going to her hardware emporium once again to spend the day having confused conversations about ratchets and voltages with the horny handed sons of toil who were its main clients. I had to admit, she seemed to be picking it up quickly. She seemed to be able to sell anything to anybody.

Occasionally a woman would wander in, looking dazed, and here Nancy came into her own.

"I need one of those thingies," the woman would say. "You know, the round ones, with the hook thing, not the flat kind." If she had picked a male member of staff, he would start pulling complicated faces in an effort not to burst out laughing, then he would say something like:

"Do you have a serial number for that, madam?"

And the customer would retreat, baffled. If she got Nancy, however, it was a different story.

"Oh, I know what you mean, yes, we've got a range of those, different colours, the yellow's my favourite, look, here they are. The flat kind are useless, actually, you're quite right to get the round one. Have you thought about getting one of these to help you assemble it? It's universal so you will use it over and over again. It's on offer at the moment too, so you're in luck..."

I had seen her in action, and also bought things in a daze myself, so I knew how this worked. It was very impressive. If I had had any more money, I would have a whole shedful of tools I never used.

I was going back to the accounts department, fortunately for my sanity for the last time. I kept my head down and inputted my data and transferred my files and updated my electronic record and then inputted more data all the time trying to filter out Suzanne's seduction techniques until I was on the verge of breakdown over the pointlessness of existence, and at this precise moment the phone rang.

"I am transferring a call to you," it was Martine's voice, "as you know we do not permit personal calls during work, I have put this one through because it is your doctor. Please keep it brief."

It was Helena.

"You're not my doctor!"

"No. I had to say something to that bossy woman. What is she, the Gestapo? Just ringing to chat through some options," she said breezily.

"I can't just now -"

"Oh, of course you can. Now, we've had to change the area of France from the one you requested."

"But - I like that area because it's cheap - I've thought a lot about it. And -"

"It's a lovely area we're going to, you'll love it. The thing is, the film crew are already on their way there."

"Oh well, we don't want to inconvenience them."

"Of course. So, you want somewhere to run - what - bird watching courses?"

"That kind of thing," I said icily. "What's wrong with bird watching?"

"Isn't it a bit - anoraky?"

"If it is, it won't be for much longer. It's going to be sexy."

"Sexy, eh? A sexy birdwatcher. Ok, I expect we can work that in. What about bird flu?"

"You're not writing the script, are you?" I was suddenly anxious.

"No, someone else does that. I'm just trying to find your perfect property. So have to make a few notes."

"So what part of France are we going to?"

"Didn't I say? Provence."

"Provence? That's really expensive."

"Like I said, the film crew are on their way there."

"You did say."

"Relax, Holly, and tell me what you want in a house. I need to get on the case."

I relaxed, and spent the next twenty minutes chattering to Helena about desirable property features. It was only a TV show, after all. Suddenly, I became aware of another presence in the room. It was Martine.

"So - this is your doctor?" she said. Uh-oh. I was in trouble.

I had lost count of the times Martine had told me never to darken her doors again. Now I was banned not just from the call centre but from the entire building. The relief at the thought that I would never have to listen to Suzanne flirting ever again was greater than my fear of starving to death through lack of paid employment. I went cheerfully back to the job centre, thank goodness I didn't have to wait hours for buses any more, and hunted among the cards for a suitable opportunity for an experienced temp. Hoorah! There was a vacancy at the call centre where Jimmy, Naz and Jen worked - my dear young friends, as

Nancy called them.

I started on Monday, after an uneventful weekend during which I hardly saw Nancy as she raced from one job to the next.

Anders didn't ring, but then I didn't exactly expect him to - I just thought - or rather I just tried not to think - oh bother. But the lovely spiky-haired young people were so welcoming, and so interested in my story about being on the telly with Goodfun, that the day went by in a flash. In fact soon I stopped thinking about Carla, Anders and mysterious men in unattractive and unfashionable jackets because I became aware of something infinitely more important, namely: what was I going to wear on the telly? It was Jen who pointed out the obvious.

"They say the telly puts pounds on you. And all those presenters are really really thin. Like anorexic. Wotcha gonna wear, Holly?"

Up to this point, I hadn't even thought about it! How could I not have thought about it? I must have been mad! AND stupid! At the end of the day, I was the first person in the car park.

"Nancy," I panted, running in through the door after a record breaking home-from-work time, "quick, we have to get new clothes."

"What, now?"

"Late night shopping at the designer outlet. Quick, quick, get in the car."

"But -"

"But nothing - I'll feed you there, you can read in the car, bring your favourite CD, anything -"

"But I want to watch Hollyoaks!"

"Tough. I'm doing you a favour, breaking your addiction. Come on, I'm offering to buy you new clothes. And shoes!"

"Oh, alright, if it's shoes as well," she said, heaving herself off the sofa.

We drove like maniacs to the designer outlet. Well, I drove, but Nancy encouraged me.

"Faster!"

"Was that a police car?"

"What will the weather be like?"

"Hot, but it might rain, you know, one of those Mediterranean storms-"

"Ooooh, Mediterranean..."

"I know!"

I should have remembered that buying new clothes for Nancy was a massive undertaking. I should have recalled the hours spent in shoe shops arguing about school shoes, suitability, and acceptability to teachers of. Now I remembered.

"But, Nancy, you're going to have to be able to walk in them!"

"Not much, I won't, only up and down in front of the camera. The rest of the time I'll be in the car, won't I!"

"You might have to do more than that. We don't know what they're going to make us do."

"Then I'll take them off between shots, and wear a different pair. I like these shoes, I don't like any of the flat ones. Anyway I look nice in these."

"Oh God. I'm going to look for something for me, I can't take any more of this."

"You can't take any more?" she yelled after me.

A little while later, in Margaret Howell, where I was trying on stripy tops and long shorts, tres continentale, she came pattering in with a carrier bag.

"I bought them myself, with my own money, so there."

"You'd better let me get you some flip flops then. For when you have blisters."

"And you can't wear stripes."

"Are you saying I look fat?"

"No, it's a telly thing, remember? They said no stripes. Interferes with the picture or something."

"Oh yes. What about the navy?"

"I think they quite like stripes. Sailors look lovely in them."

"Ha ha. The top. Non-stripy."

"No, it's too dull. Something brighter. French Connection."

"I'm not having rude slogans on my chest."

"I promise no rude slogans."

Eventually we had an acceptable outfit or two apiece, and something for the evening.

"We're going to look fab. I wonder if we'll get offers?"

"What kind of offers?"

"Oh, I don't know - modelling contracts?"

Anxiety gripped me once again as it occurred to me that this was, indeed, a possibility.

"You might get eager old men who want to marry you," she went on.

"Enough of your old men. You're obsessed with old men. Shut up and get in the car."

We drove home peacefully, as Nancy was, or was pretending to be, asleep.

Chapter 12

French Safe?

Before we knew where we were, we were in another car, heading for the airport. My period had started the previous evening, which was good, because it meant that I wasn't incubating any Rogerspawn, but bad because it was highly inconvenient while travelling. I was wearing the most comfortable pair of jeans I owned, which made me look like the back end of a pantomime elephant.

"Where are we? Are we nearly there?" asked Nancy, waking up. We had set off at four o'clock in the morning, an hour with which Nancy was not normally acquainted unless it was at the end of a particularly successful evening.

"Yes, we're nearly there, ten minutes if that. I just got a text from Guillaume to say he will meet us at the airport."

"Guillaume? Who's he?"

"He's going to be looking after us. Our every whim will be his delight. He will be Jeeves to our Wooster."

"Cool."

One uneventful flight later (apart from a star turn by the world's campest flight attendant, who had raised the emergency exit demonstration to the status of an art form, and threw the breakfasts at us with a wrist action a professional discus thrower would have envied), we stumbled blearily into the Provencal light to be met by the most beautiful man in the world, as if a Greek statue of Adonis had leapt nimbly from his plinth and gone to work in the media, for a lark. It was a good job the world's campest flight attendant wasn't there, or there might have been some kind of incident.

"I am Guillaume," he said, rather unnecessarily, as we had worked it out. "You 'ave your bags?"

We followed him, in a daze, to the car; sadly it was not the limo of our fevered imaginations but a lemon yellow Renault Clio. Guillaume slid into the front seat in a fluid motion which suggested that he was meant for nobler forms of transport. We were driven under a robin's egg blue sky past endless fields of vines and sunflowers, alternating with orchards of peaches, oranges and olives. Little streams trickled past dilapidated watermills, rows of poplars lined the roads, violet hills filled the gap between the horizon and the cloudless heavens. It was amazing. The sun shone like Nancy's fury. It was perfect. We were too dozy to chat much, so after a few half-hearted attempts at conversation, we nodded off.

We were rudely awakened, a few moments later, by what we learnt was French hip-hop.

"You never 'ear this before?"

"No, Guillaume, never. In England we don't get to hear a lot of continental hip-hop, as it happens."

"It's good, no?"

"Gosh, what can I say?"

"You like it?"

"I don't normally like hip-hop," Nancy said tactfully, "but it sounds - more interesting in French."

"Everything sounds better in French," Guillaume laughed. He threw his head back, and, from my seat in the back, I could see his perfect teeth in the driving mirror. Gosh, he really was pretty.

"Is there anything you need to know about your stay? Come on, ask me, I can answer anything."

"Well, I've been wondering, who does our make-up?" I asked.

There was a lot more laughter and display of perfect teeth before Guillaume could answer that one.

"You do."

"Us? But aren't there wardrobe people and stuff? We can't do our own make-up, we'll look terrible."

"Sorry, no. It's all down to you. You know you have to wear the same clothes all week?"

"What?"

"Yes, it 'as to look as if we do all the shoot in one day, so you wear the same clothes."

"But -"

"No-one ever explains this," Guillaume said, as if to himself, shaking his head sadly.

"Always people think there is going to be make-up artists and limousines and champagne. And truffles and armagnac. Pate de fois gras and feux d'artifice. No, no, it is not like this at all, even the presenters do their own make-up. This is not the glamorous life you think, you know. It is illusion, you understand? Television." As if to confirm this, we arrived at our hotel, which was disappointingly ordinary, and could have been in a depressing suburb of Leeds were it not for the intense light which cruelly emphasised its distressed concrete façade All those cracks. It was probably fortysomething. I empathised with its struggle to remain in any way alluring. Hotel des Arbres, it announced, and it was in fact true that a couple of saplings were struggling to survive in the car park.

"I thought we were going to be fabulous TV stars?" Nancy hissed at me, as we ascended in the grey carpeted lift.

"Well shoot me for a fraudulent misrepresentation of fact."

"When I get you home, I will. Under English law." There was malevolence in her eyes. I began to have grave doubts about our mission.

I have video evidence of our trip to France, provided by Goodfun Productions after our return, but it bears little resemblance to what actually happened. It shows a mother and daughter, looking with enthusiastic, cheerful interest round a number of properties all in one day, and filling in any spare time (they seem to have a lot of spare time) with interesting visits to museums, lavender oil distilleries and wine tastings. They have witty and pertinent remarks to make about everything, and they laugh heartily at the presenter's jokes, which he makes (spontaneously) every two minutes. While it is true that we had some terrific times, the tape entirely fails to show the truth. So this chapter will tell you the truth about reality television - just in case you ever, after a few glasses of Rioja, find yourself seated at the computer and composing an email to a production company. It may be your toddlers, your teenagers, your spouse, your house or merely your décor - the temptation to get the experts in to sort you out (on film) can be overwhelming in certain circumstances (like being a bit drunk). All I can say to you is, don't do it unless you really, really want to be on telly. Don't do it if you really, really want them to sort your life out. It's television. It's not going to sort your life out. Only you can do that. With a little help from books like this, of course.

On Day One, we were driven at dawn for an hour and a half into the middle of nowhere and shown a totally unsuitable house in a deplorable state which needed rebuilding entirely. It also had very close neighbours who kept a large dog which barked continually (until the owners were bribed by Guillaume to shut him up) and, we discovered, to the horror of Nancy, also kept hundreds of battery rabbits. And I don't mean the pink, cymbal-banging kind you get in adverts. I mean the kind you eat.

"Look!" she shrieked, as she wandered past the open barn door while we were waiting for the crew to set up their shots, "How cruel! poor little things!"

"You used to keep your rabbit in a cage, well a hutch," I pointed out in a low voice,

"Poppy didn't mind at all."

"That's because I used to get her out EVERY day and let her play on the lawn! And I wasn't planning to EAT her!" Nancy's voice was still quite penetrating.

"The thing is, farmers don't see their animals in that way, they're not so sentimental -" Oops, wrong word.

"Sentimental! I'm not sentimental, I just care, not like all these horrible people, I hate farmers and I hate French people and nothing will make me change my mind. In fact, I don't want you to move to France now so there's no point in doing this stupid programme, is there?" And with that she started to remove her microphone. Harriet, the producer, came hurrying over. The sound man, who had received our exchange through his headphones (I had seen him wincing), had tipped her off that all was not well.

"All ready," she beamed anxiously. "Nancy, you need to keep that on, my love, so we can hear what you say."

"I don't want to do it any more." Nancy's eyes were extra bright with tears that were dammed against her lower lashes.

"Of course you do, my darling, and we're going to such a lovely place for lunch, they do the best ice cream you ever ever tasted."

Nancy hesitated, and the tears receded.

"What flavours?"

"Which is your favourite?"

"Mint choc chip," Nancy said, sounding about six.

"I'm not sure if they have it, shall I get Guillaume to ring them and ask?"

"Yes, please," said Nancy in a very small voice.

"Good," said Harriet, briskly, "now, we need you over here and you and Robbie can go through what you're going to say. But remember, we need you to be spontaneous. Guillaume, ring the restaurant and find out what flavours of ice cream they have. Now, please. Immediately."

Guillaume slouched languidly and sexily off to make the phone call, and soon all that could be seen of him was a plume of cigarette smoke behind a dry stone wall. Beyond him, the beautiful valley dropped away in an early morning haze and the terraced hills reared on either side. Cypresses speared through the mist and buzzards circled and called below us. The view was the only good thing about the house, as I did not fail to point out on film. Nancy went on about the rabbits, which made her feel a lot better ("got to make a stand, mum") but this was edited out of the final version, needless to say. We did everything at least three times. We walked into a room, we said, ooh, gosh, look at the fireplace, we pointed at the broken tiles, the rotting beams and the shocking state of the electrics. Then we went out, and came in again, and said it all again. Spontaneously. Then we did it again, from different angles. Then we did noddies. This was where we nodded, for close ups. We did long shots, in which we walked about, and it didn't matter what we said, so Robbie, the presenter ("Guillaume! Where's the gay paint? I've got a spot!") tried to shock us with outrageous remarks. I became slightly indignant.

"It's hopeless! I couldn't possibly do what I want to do, here!"

"Yes, but it's very photogenic."

"But I really thought you might find me a house," I said sadly.

"It's TV, love," Robbie said, patting we on the head.

Harriet continued to impress me with her Nancy-managing ability. I was fairly sure she would have rebelled by now if I was trying to get her to do all these silly things three times in a row. But Nancy continued to perform, occasionally with a secret smile on her face, which worried me.

Finally, we did perv cam. This was where we looked as if Nancy and I were having a private conversation about the house (artfully arranged vegetation between us and the camera adding to the illusion) but the film crew had crept up on us and sneakily caught our candid remarks. Most of this got cut, as it consisted largely of Nancy's views on French attitudes to animal cruelty.

We packed up at lunch time by which time I was completely exhausted and jumped straight into the car where I lay full length on the back seat waiting for lovely Guillaume to transport us to the restaurant. The weather, which had been misty first thing, was now, at midday, radiantly hot. I think I may have dozed, briefly.

I was half dreaming about a perfect life in France, meals outdoors on the terrace round an old rustic table spread with a white linen cloth (picked up cheap at the marché des puces) and laid with charmingly unmatched old crockery and glasses. In the centre a posy of wildflowers provided the finishing touch. The guests were all laughing and happily chatting about the lovely day they had had, and I was swishing about in a long frock and a straw hat, bringing dishes of glorious food to the table...

Suddenly, Nancy leapt into the car, almost landing on my face. I sat up, quickly. Guillaume was in the front, with Harriet, and the van with the crew and Robbie was preceding us up the track ahead.

"Sorry," Nancy said, "let's go! I was looking at this butterfly, mum," she explained.

"It was really beautiful, sort of yellow and black, and I almost forgot where I was." The car started off. I looked out of the back window, for one last glimpse of the wonderful view. What was all that stuff, moving? The ground was alive. It was heaving what was going on? I opened my mouth to exclaim, but Nancy kicked me so hard that I turned to look at her instead. She was frowning, meaningfully. Meaning what? As we neared the bend, I looked round once more and light dawned.

It was all the rabbits. I fully expected this deed to catch up with Nancy, but we heard no more about it. Later that evening, when we were finally alone, I half-heartedly told her off.

"In any case, the farmer will have rounded them all up and put them back in the cages. So it was rather pointless. Honestly, Nancy. Not very grown up."

"Some of them will have got away. And those few will have children, and tell them about the evil farmer, and they'll multiply and possibly mutate and then one day they'll all go to the farm in an army and find him and kill him!"

"I see."

We slept really well after our busy day, and the next morning we set off even earlier to see another house. This one was in a town and there was the usual wait while the crew set up the shots so we went off to explore, and buy presents. It was a nice, typically French town, and we wandered happily through the squares and streets, past little cafés and charcuteries, boulangeries and - to Nancy's great delight - a quincaillerie. She took a photo so that she could send it to work.

"I'm going to find hardware stores all over the world, when I go travelling."

This remark made my blood run a bit cold, but I comforted myself with the thought that this day was a long way off. At least two years. I could spend the time in between, adjusting to the idea of Nancy travelling the world, defenceless. We wandered into lots of shops and bought totally unsuitable things. Nancy bought mostly edible presents, and I doubted whether many of them would reach their intended recipients, but tactfully refrained from making any remark to this effect. I bought a large straw hat (which was exactly like the one I had imagined, but was to prove to be an awkward traveller) and some striped, hand made bowls and plates.

"When I get my new French house, I'll have these on display in the kitchen."

Nancy said nothing, but her facial expression was not encouraging, I think. Soon we were summoned by Guillaume and went to see the town house. Arranged over five floors, including a massive cellar complex, it was definitely big enough to accommodate a lot of people. It was also in a reasonable state of repair, though it all needed decorating. It had huge rooms with shutters on the windows and marble fireplaces.

"I've asked a local builder for some estimates," Robbie warbled for the camera (he had done no such thing, what else were researchers for?), "and it seems like we're looking at two thousand pounds if you want to knock these walls down and open the space up a bit, for your school."

"Are there a lot of birds round here?" I asked, innocently, and Robbie scowled at me, turning away from the camera to do so, because we were on a very busy road through the town and the sound man was having huge problems every time a lorry thundered by, as was the cameraman, because they blotted out the light.

"There's a garden at the back," he said, "why don't you both follow me?" but in fact it was not until several takes and three quarters of an hour later that we made it into the garden, which was a pleasant, walled rectangle about thirty feet by twenty. It was rather sweet. There was, to be fair, a blackbird in the lilac bush.

"So, what do we think?" Robbie said cheerfully, rubbing his hands.

"I think it's a no," I said.

"So do I," said Nancy.

"The road," I added. "Not very conducive to quiet contemplation."

Apparently, this let us out of perv cam, because we weren't even going to consider it, so we got home early. The crew were going to film the expensive "hot prop" in the area (seven million pounds, apparently) and so Nancy and I spent the afternoon in the hotel swimming pool.

"God, mum," she said, surfacing after an underwater length of the pool, "this is the business. I wish it was all like this."

"So you like some things about France, then?"

"I like the weather. And the birds. The people are horrible."

"You like Guillaume. And the waiter who gave you an extra pain au chocolat for breakfast. And the old lady in the bar who started singing."

"Well apart from them. Most of the people are just nasty."

We floated for a while. Then suddenly, from nowhere, Nancy began to cry.

"What is it?"

I got her out of the pool, and we sat side by side on a sun lounger, where she sobbed.

"I'm just homesick, I think," she said eventually, when she could speak.

I was not at all convinced that this was all it was, but now was not the time to push for explanations. That would have to wait. I wondered if she was going down with something. She was always grumpy when she was sickening. For now, lots of comforting was all I could do. It seemed to be enough.

Finally, on day three, we found the house of my dreams. When we first glimpsed it, from the road, I couldn't believe that we were in the right place, as it was too good to be true. I suspected that it was out of my price range.

The house was set above the road, with some trees screening it from the prevailing winds. Above were mountains, down the road was a gorge where reputedly vultures and eagles were to be found. The whole property was surrounded by lavender fields. It was perfect. As usual, we had to hang around outside while the crew faffed about setting up their shots.

"Sodding Harriet thinks she's sodding Fellini," I grumbled impatiently, keen to get inside. The gentle breeze played with the leaves of the chestnut tree above our heads, and a lizard scuttled into a crack in the wall. Here was the perfect place for my outdoor table. The house, I could see from the outside, had a beautiful, ancient barn (to convert?) attached as well as the main house, which looked very substantial. The whole complex, apparently having sprung directly out of the land on which it sat, was built of a beautiful, creamy grey limestone which was like the stone I saw every day in Wharfedale. The front of the house and the barn formed a continuous line of rough stone wall, like a cliff face studded with blue, typically provencal doors and windows. The drive up to the house was a concern, as it was narrow and deeply rutted with a sharp turn to the left which, I foresaw, would present problems to any large vehicle (such as, for example, a removal van) which attempted it.

But these minor problems were only obstacles to be overcome it appeared that I had found The House. My heart thudded. I was in love.

"What do you think?"

"I think, bloody hell!"

"You can come in now!" Harriet called. Robbie came down the steps, as we needed to be seen going up to the front door.

"Let's not drag this out," he said, grinning. "It's a great house. Let's do this in one take, then we can get inside. Just need Guillaume with the gay paint again."

Guillaume hastened over with the concealer.

"And - action," shouted Harriet.

"So - Holly - what are your first impressions?" Robbie asked, as he preceded us up the stairs.

"I'm overwhelmed, Robbie," I said, truthfully as it happened.

"Look at the keys to this place," he went on, brandishing the kind of key you use to lock a church, "these could be yours. It's an eighteenth century farmhouse, what are your thoughts, Nancy?"

"I think it's wonderful," Nancy said, to my enormous relief, as I suspected we had done enough for the shot. And indeed it was, because Harriet graciously allowed us into the kitchen, for the next bit.

"What are your thoughts in here?"

"I can just see that this would be a great place to congregate in the evenings, to discuss the birds or the photographs or the poems or whatever people had been doing. I can see us all sitting around a big table, eating great food, if the weather was too cold for us to be outside - it's just perfect, Robbie -" and with that I turned to him, buried my face in his designer shirt and burst into tears.

Harriet was overjoyed, even if Robbie had now got mascara all over his shirt. It was the money shot. They continued to film until I stopped.

There was a slightly unpleasant voyeuristic feeling in the room.

"And cut. That'll do for in here," Harriet said.

"Well I certainly couldn't cry again, so I hope you don't want to try that again." I said firmly, wiping my eyes. "Can I put some more make-up on?"

Robbie and Guillaume were fussing over Robbie's shirt so we all had a break for a few minutes, and happily for me they let me go into the rooms that weren't being filmed. There were five beautiful bedrooms, all with perfect views (all the windows in the house enjoyed views of mountains, lavender fields, the river in the valley, the woods clinging to the hillsides and following the course of the river, and the hilltop village in the distance). There were fireplaces, beams, a wonderful garden, even a spout where a spring should gush into a stone basin below, though the spring was unfortunately dry. This was one of the only things which struck doubt into my heart which otherwise entirely belonged to the darling house. It was all a bit too Jean de Florette.

"Why is there no water in the spring?" I asked Guillaume.

"I don't know. We could ask the agent."

Now I was introduced to a person I had noticed in the background, but not really registered. He was Patrick (pronounced PatReek with the emphasis on the Reek), the agent. I was immediately annoyed by the fact that he was French and had an Irish name.

"Do you have family from Ireland?" I asked. I was talking French, because Patreek didn't speak English at all (luckily I had got my call centre practice in), but I am translating for the benefit of readers whose French isn't as good as mine. Ahem.

"No, not at all," he answered smoothly and unapologetically.

"So why do you have an Irish name?"

Patreek looked surprised. "Because my mother likes it," he replied. I wanted to roll my eyes sarcastically at this, but refrained, as I was aware that I might have to negotiate with the man at a later stage. He was a bit younger than me, oily, with slicked back black hair and a cashmere sweater slung casually round his shoulders. And slip-on shoes, that hallmark of the unreliable. He clearly believed himself to be almost irresistibly good-looking. He was very annoying indeed. I disliked him at first sight.

"Why is there no water in the spring?" I demanded.

Patreek shrugged his shoulders and held out his hands in a helpless yet all-embracing gesture.

"Who knows where the water moves? Maybe she is blocked, maybe it is because we have had dry weather. I feel sure that she will flow again, if she is treated with love."

This kind of thing was no help at all, so I went back to work, and we got through the takes, the noddies, the long shots and perv cam with minimum fuss. Harriet was very pleased with us.

"Well done, everybody," she enthused, I think this is going to be a really good show. Are you interested in making an offer, Holly?"

"I am." I was. Guillaume and I went off with the agent to negotiate, and it was agreed that Robbie would pretend to do it for me, on film, the next day when we went back for our second viewing.

The agent had a (predictably) very flashy office where he installed us in comfy chairs and got minions to fetch coffee while he got out lots of bits of paper. Harriet had given me a list of "Buying a house in France - dos and don'ts" and Guillaume was there so I felt reasonably confident. I was a tough, self-sufficient woman who spoke French - in her own way and at her own speed - I could handle this. Yikes! What the hell was I doing?

"So, what offer do you want to make?"

The asking price had been outside my budget, so I needed the price to come down a bit. I had discussed it with Harriet and she had said more than 10I took a deep breath, and offered two hundred and ten thousand pounds. With agent's fees and taxes, this meant I would be spending nearly all my money and there would be nothing left for improvements and putting a roof on the barn. But it was a once in a lifetime opportunity, it was perfect and people would flock (no pun intended) to my courses...

Patreek wrote down my offer, looking as if I was a bit of a disappointment to him. The corners of his mouth turned down briefly, in an "oh, well," kind of way. We signed things. I said it was conditional on a survey and at that Patreek looked astounded. He pushed his chair back and braced both hands on the desk as if he were in the presence of a lunatic and might have to fight. His eyebrows went up into his oily hair. Luckily Guillaume stepped in at this point and explained that in England, people insisted on these weird things called structural surveys.

"But you can see with your own eyes that the house is good," Patreek protested, waving his hands as though feeling the invisible buttocks of a large person about to sit on his lap.

"Nevertheless," I insisted.

"It has been there for hundreds of years. I assure you, it is not going to fall down just now."

Eventually we got away and Guillaume drove me back to the hotel. He said he was very pleased for me, though I thought this was probably because it made better television. That night we all went out to celebrate.

"It's a really fabulous house, darling," Harriet said to me over the aperitifs (she was already a bit tipsy), "and what you're going to do with it is just great. I just know you'll make a great success of it. You know we get a lot of people on this show who scare me a lot. They rush into projects when they don't speak the language, they don't understand the culture, they just see a cheap property and they get all greedy. You're not like that. I think you'll be fine."

"Yes," Guillaume broke in, "remember that couple in Hungary? Oh my God - that was terrible - there was everything wrong with that house, it was a disaster. They wanted to turn it into a brothel, I think, but they never said it on camera of course."

"I thought they were swingers, didn't you?" said Harriet, "he came on to me and made some pretty lewd suggestions, actually."

"Oh, I had that too," said Guillaume casually. "It happens I went to her room one evening, she had a very nice top on, sort of pink and see-through and she looked very sexy, and then just when we were getting started he came in wearing a cowboy hat, I was panicking, I think he will kill me, but he wants to join in."

"What did you do?"

"It all get a bit hazy after that. I think we must have taken something."

"I think Guillaume is a bit of a bad influence," Harriet said privately to me. "Don't leave him on his own with Nancy."

I looked around. Where was Nancy? She had left the table, gone to the toilet I supposed.

"What does Nancy think about the house?"

"She loves the house, not so sure about the country surrounding it."

"The lavender fields?"

"France."

"Oh. Disillusioned?"

"She's only young."

We both sighed. Harriet was younger than I was, but not much. Unlike me, she had sacrificed family life on the altar of her brilliant media career. And here she was, making daytime reality TV. Oh dear.

"Do you feel you made the right choices in life, Harriet?" I was a bit tipsy, too.

"God knows. What are the right choices, anyway? I didn't want babies and that nonsense when I was young. Thought it was for losers - no offence -"

"None taken."

"Not so sure now, am I?"

"It's not fair, men don't have to make these decisions."

"No, they can just marry a twenty something when they're fifty, if they've got enough money to tempt one."

"Have you never been married, Harriet?"

"No, never wanted to, if I'm honest. Never met the right man."

I suddenly noticed that Guillaume had left the table and that Nancy had still not returned.

"You don't think - he wouldn't -" I spluttered, leaping up and running to the toilets.

I found Nancy sobbing in one of the cubicles in the Ladies.

"Oh, thank God, I thought Guillaume was giving you cocaine."

"Never mind that I'm upset, then."

"No, no, of course I mind, it's just that my imagination was running riot."

"Oh good, well it can stop then, can't it."

"Why are you so upset? I told you, I won't move here until you go to uni, or whatever you decide at eighteen. And you can always come here and stay, you know that. What's the problem?"

"Oh, I don't know mum, I expect I'm being silly. Let's go back and eat something, eh?" We sat down at the table and Nancy glowered at those members of our party who had foolishly ordered the pate de foie gras. Unfortunately, as if this wasn't enough, rabbit with prunes was one of the mains, and the cameraman and Harriet both had it. Nancy's mood, already dark, was plummeting down the roller coaster of woe towards blackest night.

I was chatting to Harriet about Carla, and how I was worried that something bad had happened to her, when Nancy suddenly broke into our conversation.

"Oh, yes," she said, angrily breaking bits of bread and scattering them on the table as she spoke, "you care about her don't you? You've only just met her but you've got enough time to spend on her, worrying about her, going out drinking with her. What about me? When do you spend time with me? Your daughter?"

"Every evening," I said, trying to sound calm, "I come home and cook your tea and chat to you about school."

"But when do you spend proper time with me? Going to see a film or something?"

"I'm spending all this week with you."

"Oh, great! Big treat!"

She was shouting now and the rest of the room had gone quiet.

"Anyway," she said, appearing to calm down slightly, and speaking in a quiet, controlled voice, "I just thought that you ought to know. I'm sleeping with my English teacher."

Silence fell upon the room, apart from the susurration of non-English speakers whispering to their more linguistically adept fellow diners, to ask what did she just say? Or rather, qu'est-ce qu'elle a dit? Mon dieu.

"What? Which one?" I said stupidly, unable to visualise her English teacher.

"Graeme. Mr Birch."

"Oh God!"

"I've been babysitting for him, and afterwards, when he brings me home, we stop somewhere."

"Oh my God - Rita Sue and Bob too! The little shit!"

"What? There isn't anyone else. Look, I just couldn't bear to carry on lying to you. So, there it is. I'm telling you the truth, you should be pleased, I would have thought."

"What am I going to do?" I appealed to the table. Everyone had an opinion. Robbie thought he should be reported to the police, immediately, in fact he was getting his phone out but Nancy began to scream so he put it away again, but continued to mutter.

"Accessory after the fact," he murmured occasionally. (Robbie had a law degree and had been "in commercial property" before he had been lured into the spangled maw of showbiz.)

Harriet thought I should go and confront him in person, and offered to send a camera crew with me for "moral support."

The cameraman had a friend who knew an ex-policeman who would wire brush him, for a fee. Apparently this process involved the removal of the victim's clothes followed by vigorous application of a wire brush to all parts, particularly between the legs. This was very tempting, and I resolved to get the number when Nancy was out of earshot which as it fell out was quite soon, as Nancy now decided to become hysterical, possibly at the thought of Graeme getting a sound wire brushing, and run out of the restaurant, into the black, French night. We all ran after her but she had disappeared, so everyone scattered in different directions. I ran down an alley, shouting her name in a panicky voice that didn't sound like mine. Once again I was feeling like the world's worst mother. How did this keep happening?

I've been neglecting her, I thought as I ran, I've not been putting her first, all the time, I've been out with men - Suddenly I stopped running. Two things had happened. It had just occurred to me that I was not a bad mother at all, and that another, quite differently gendered parent was the one doing the neglecting, which was presumably why old men suddenly looked attractive to poor Nancy. And, in addition, I had heard a familiar snuffling noise, reminiscent of a baby pig searching for a tasty titbit in deep straw, coming from behind a phone booth (which was covered with a huge poster advertising DJ Heep Hop et le Cool Extraordinaire.)

"Nancy," I said quietly, holding out my hand as if to a timid creature of the woods.

"I hate you," she (literally) spat at me.

"We have to go back to the hotel to talk about this. Let's get a cab."

"I don't want to talk to you. I just want to go home, as soon as possible."

"We're going home as soon as possible. Tomorrow."

"You just can't take anything seriously, can you? Everything's at a distance with you. You don't cry, you don't feel, you don't hurt."

"You don't see me cry."

"Is it a coincidence every time? I just happen not to be there?"

"No, I go away so you don't see me crying. I don't want to upset you."

"Well it upsets me more that you don't get upset, actually."

"OK, I'll get upset, more. Is that good? And We'll be honest with each other. And we'll discuss things. And you," I added firmly, "are going to spend some time with your dad. I think he's just the person you need at the moment."

The next morning, we assembled round the breakfast table in various woeful conditions. Nancy and I were still avoiding eye contact and had not slept very well, which had left me with dark rings under my eyes, and her paler than ever. It was lucky we weren't filming, as it would have needed a lot of amateurishly applied make-up. Over our pains au chocolat, we heard what had happened to the others. Harriet, drifting slightly drunkenly into an interesting part of town, had wandered into a lesbian club and said she was looking for a girl, whereupon several interesting developments had kept her out most of the night. She was looking quite pleased with herself, and talking about doing a documentary on the subject.

"You know Holly," she said confidingly to me later, "I always wondered why I preferred oral sex. I think this could change the course of my career AND my relationships! And I'm going to look into artificial insemination!"

Robbie and the sound man had thought they'd seen a man trying to push Nancy into a car and had accosted him. It wasn't Nancy, of course, as she was with me, and so the man's friends got out of the car and helped him to give Robbie and the sound man a bit of a battering. Guillaume had come along just in time to get them to casualty, where they spent the rest of the night being stitched up.

But the prize of the night went to the camera man, who also got stitched up. He had met a man who had offered to sell him some drugs. Off they had gone together to a dark alley where the cameraman had been relieved of all his possessions including his trainers and his tee shirt (they had allowed him to keep his jeans.) Having no head for directions and no French he wandered around for most of the night, stepping in his socks in most of the dog poo in the city and crying with frustration until he was picked up by the police at five in the morning and brought back, after they had rung round all the hotels in the city to find out which one had an English TV crew staying there. Because he had forgotten the name of the hotel.

That morning, we were not a happy bunch. Which, as I remarked earlier, made it all the odder to see the lovely film they made out of our experiences.

Chapter 13

A box of assorted creams

Back in Blighty I rang Basil, whom I had thought never to see again, and filled him in on the developments in my life.

"I think I need a lot of legal help," I said.

"It's too much for one man," he said faintly, after I had explained.

"You mean - you can't - you don't - "

"I mean I have colleagues who specialise in other areas of the law," Basil said. "I think you'll need a French lawyer for the house purchase, in any case. Now, what were the other things?"

"My daughter and the evil teacher."

"Is she willing to press charges?"

"No."

"Then it's not a criminal matter. He's in breach of his professional conduct clause, of course, and he could lose his job. But she's sixteen?"

"Yes." I said reluctantly.

"I suggest you approach the school, and put things in writing. Come back to me if things get difficult."

"Alright, I'll do that. But what about my friend who's disappeared? Can I hire your private detective?"

"Do you have an interest in her disappearance?"

"She's my friend," I protested.

"Any financial interest?"

"Well, er, sort of. Not really. I mean, I lent her some money for her divorce. But there's this really shady character been hanging around, I think he's part of a plot to make her vanish. Rub her out," I added darkly, thinking this sounded suitably alarming.

"I see." He sounded far too calm, almost resigned.

"What are you saying?"

"How much did you lend her?"

"Five thousand pounds."

I could hear Basil tutting.

"I trusted her. She wouldn't take any more - I offered more. I still trust her. I think something bad might have happened -"

"I think she's taken your money and moved on. Have you got any written evidence of this loan?"

"No."

"I think you're going to have to chalk it up to experience. I'm sorry Holly, it sounds like you've been had."

But of course I didn't believe it. I knew Carla, and she wouldn't do that to me. So if Basil wouldn't help me, I would find her on my own.

I arranged for Nancy to spend some time with her father, because she wasn't really speaking to me any more, and I began to make a plan of action. I would contact everyone I knew who knew Carla, and find out if they knew anyone else who knew her. Armed with this mighty list, I would get clues, cross reference evidence, and finally discover a tell-tale Silk Cut butt and a giant satellite-shaped earring where it was least expected. I would start with Anders. What a very good place to start. Mmmm. I might have to snog him again, of course, but some sacrifices would have to be made in order to accomplish my quest, and snogging married men might be up there on the list. Oh well.

But before I could start with Anders, I had a week's work to do and I was back on the phones in a narrow, airless room furnished entirely in grey plastic, talking to very dreary people about mobile phones. At least my colleagues were lovely. Jimmy, Jen and Naz were deeply sympathetic when I told them about Nancy and the evil teacher.

"I got hit on by my history teacher when I was at school," Naz said. "He used to take me out for drinks at lunchtime, I thought I was dead cool and all my mates were jealous. I thought he liked talking to me. Then one day I was going on about some idea I'd had about Mary Queen of Scots and when I stopped talking, I asked him, cos he wasn't saying anything, what do you think? What do I think about what? he says. I said, what I just said about Mary Queen of Scots. Oh, he said, I wasn't listening, I was looking at your tits. They're fabulous, aren't they? Do they stay up by themselves, or do you have to wear a bra?"

"Bastard," we chorused, though Jimmy looked a bit thoughtful for a while.

"How old were you, Naz?" Jen asked

"Sixteen."

"That's alright, it's legal," Jimmy said but we all glared at him and he shut up.

"Changing the subject," Jen said, "we had a message for you last week, from somewhere else you used to work? Woman called Martina or something? Trying to contact you."

"Oh, I don't think we have anything else to say to each other," I said hastily. Best if I don't speak to her."

Jen shrugged. "I don't know, it might be urgent. People were running all over the shop looking for you."

"If it's really important I expect she'll manage to let me know," I said fervently hoping that she wouldn't.

I arranged to meet Anders again, to go to the same pub and interrogate the barman. I rang him on his mobile. Anders was nervous, but said he was happy to go for a drink, as long as no-one (he meant me) got aggressive or anything.

"It's all right," I assured him, "I have learnt the art of calm. I read it in a magazine. If I get stressed, I do special breathing."

"Hmm," he said, sceptically.

"But the thing is, Anders, she could have been murdered."

"It's not very likely, Holly, I think."

"I might report her missing to the police."

"I don't think you want to get into anything like that. What can the police do?"

"If a body turns up, they could match it with our description of course."

"I think you watch too much TV. The police ask you a lot of questions about you, they write it down and forget about it is what happens."

"How do you know?"

"I don't trust the police," Anders said darkly. It made me hesitate. Were all men untapped wells of corruption and depravity? Or was it just the ones I got mixed up with? I changed the subject.

"Meanwhile, I need to sort out this mess at Nancy's school. But they're on holiday at the moment, so I can't do anything. It would be so complicated. I might have to leave it."

"How long is it to wait?"

"Don't you have children, Anders?"

There was a bit of an embarrassed pause.

"Yes, two, a boy and a girl."

"So you really ought to know when the holidays are."

"Yes. The thing is -"

"What?"

"My wife has taken them back to Sweden."

"Oh - no! I'm so sorry, Anders. I was being really tactless! God! I hate myself sometimes. Honestly, I'm so so sorry!"

"It's alright. Don't worry about it."

"No, I feel awful. I'm really sorry. I'll make up for it on Friday."

And on that note, we ended our conversation. I think I meant I'd buy him a drink. I think he thought I meant sex. Oh, what the hell.

I also had to make preparations to return to France to sign all the documents which would put the seal on my perfect house. Flights, hire car and accommodation were all easily sorted out over the internet. But who could advise me about the state of the house? I was in a quandary. I was moaning about it at work.

"If only I knew a builder."

"Well..." Jimmy said.

"Don't tell me you know a builder?"

"I am a builder. Well, until I decided there was more money in working in a call centre, I used to work for me dad, now he still is a builder. Nothing I don't know about the trade. My dad started taking me out to sites when I was eleven."

"Do you want to come to France with me? All expenses paid?"

"Is the pope catholic?"

"I believe so. Also the sky is blue, especially in Provence. And the pope used to live there."

"I'm not going if you're going to try and educate us."

"Alright I won't. I won't mention anything educational the whole time we're there."

"Can we have snails?"

"Why not?"

"You know, Holly," Jen said, "Jimmy isn't the lovely sweet boy he appears to be."

"Of course he is."

We were all just joshing.

The night before I flew to France with Jimmy, I slept with Anders. It happened like this. We went to the same pub as before and spoke to the same morose barman.

"Only wants an ouse in Croatia now, says it's the new otspot, saw it on some TV programme about buying ouses abroad."

"Oh," I piped up brightly, "I went on a progr- , er," I hesitated as I reconsidered this potentially antagonistic conversational gambit, "as it happens I went to Croatia once on a, er, holiday, before they had the war of course."

"Before the war? You must be a lot older than you look, lass."

"Not that war - oh I decided not to go any further down this line. I needed to be direct, so I decided to just rush in and mention Carla again."

"My Italian friend," I began, and didn't need to go any further because this time he put down the grubby tea towel with which he had been unenthusiastically polishing the pumps and leaned over the bar, breathing a confiding odour of rotten teeth in our direction. Anders recoiled, but I, determined to find the truth, remained rooted to my post.

"She were a bad 'un. You know that chap what were in 'ere last time you was askin about er? E ad a bad time with that un. She told im to go after some old bird what she worked with, try to get er to go out wiv im, said she ad loads o money."

"Really?"

"Aye, but t'other old bird twigged what were goin on, so e says. Anyway, she's tekken money off people and legged it, e reckons. Probably not the first time. I bet she never paid no rent neither. I 'ate people like that, ruddy foreign scroungers. Bloody good job she's legged it, if you ask me, I'd not be very nice to 'er if I saw 'er again. Good bloody riddance. Bloody foreigners. Asylum seekers and the like. So called migrant workers, tekkin our jobs. Can't be doin wi' em."

I was a bit perplexed by all this, as it confirmed what I'd heard before. Could Carla really have asked Miami Vice to ask me out? Why would she do that? It was all very confusing. But the one thing I was clear about was that I still believed in Carla. Presumably another example of my utter cluelessness where people and their motivation was concerned. Look at Roger. And Nancy. I was hopeless.

Anders, naturally, had heard all this and was trying to look concerned while unsuccessfully repressing his sniggers.

"Alright, ha ha," I said.

"If it's any consolation, I don't think you're an old bird."

"Great."

"So was he good looking, this man?"

"We saw him, last time we were here."

"Oh dear. Carla doesn't have a very high opinion of your attractiveness, I think. You can do much better than that."

"Really? What do you think about my attractiveness?" (My ego was deflated, that's my only excuse).

"The first time I saw you, I thought you were outstandingly attractive. Since then, increased exposure to you has only confirmed my opinion."

"Gosh, Anders, your English is good. Do you practice these phrases often?"

"No."

"I'm sorry." I thought he might be offended but actually he was just using it as an excuse to look burningly into my eyes and grab my hand. Oooh he was sexy.

"I'm serious, Holly," he said. "I'm really crazy about you."

"Hmmm," I said, overwhelmed with desire, "I don't suppose you want to come home for coffee?"

"I do, actually."

He did, actually. And then - well, I already told you what happened then.

****

But then - the next morning - I felt terrible. He was married. It was like sleeping with a man, a woman, and his assorted children about whom I had been extremely anxious to know nothing. Also he had left straight away after we finished so he could perhaps get home to his wife, who may or may not have been in Sweden with the children, and I had this sinking feeling that he would never call and would never want to see me again. And this suspicion proved to be entirely correct.

But I forgot about all this disastrous episode in my life as a few days later I embarked on yet another one, flying to France with a young man I barely knew, to buy a house I had seen only twice, and that with a TV crew in tow. I had ordered a tiny little hire car from the airport but had never actually driven a left hand drive car before, so was concealing a secret terror of changing gear with my right hand, which I suspected was impossible. Jimmy was no help at all.

We drove out of the airport in a flurry of him telling me what to do and me telling him to shut the fuck up as the gears ground hideously in complaint. It was a long drive. By the time we reached the bed and breakfast I had booked online ("charming farmhouse accommodation with en-suite facilities, serving local produce" - actually a collection of concrete outbuildings with on-site pack of hounds which miraculously appeared milling around the doorway every time we went in or out of the room) we were no longer speaking at all, and the engine was producing a hot, impatient oily smell. However - later that night - after a lovely meal in the local restaurant - with snails - we made up in a way I hadn't totally anticipated - Jimmy being so much younger than me and all that I was still working on the assumption that ours was a purely platonic relationship. Blah blah blah.

Oh, who was I kidding? Jen was right, and he wasn't just a lovely sweet boy. Our room was at the back of the house, and had a stunning view. That was its best feature. That and the fact that we had two double beds. Madame - our hostess - was unable to spare us a lot of time what with running the farm (goats, sheep, and something mysterious growing in the fields), feeding the dogs, driving the dogs out of the way with a broom, smoking incessantly and taking her grandson out for walks in his buggy down the rutted track which led to the village. So although I kept trying to catch her attention, she was never there so I could point out to her that the bedside lights didn't work, the window was dirty, the toilet didn't flush properly, there was something brown smeared on the wallpaper and the curtains didn't close properly. Anyway, I was distracted.

For the second time in less than a week I fucked a man who was so totally unsuitable that it looked as though I was on a quest for Mr Wrong. What was I doing? My self-esteem was on the floor. I had no self respect. I was just a disaster. Oh woe and despair. On the other hand: sleeping with Jimmy was just the most gorgeous thing. I quite understood, after that, why men like younger women so much. His energy! His lovely smooth skin! His enthusiasm! His recovery time! I won't go on. As I said earlier, it'll only get you all hot and bothered. And anyway, you need to find these things out for yourself. I dare you.

The next day (after morning sex, twice!) we arrived at the house before the agent did, so without the key Jimmy and I wandered around looking at the outside, I pointed out the lovely features, the barn, the lavender fields, the views. It was even better than I remembered. A pair of buzzards turned lazily in the sky above us, and Jimmy took my hand. Crickets leapt chirruping out of the grass and thistles ahead of us as we strode through the thigh-high wilderness which was the land belonging to the house. I could visualise rows of vegetables for healthy home-cooked meals and places for my visitors to play jolly garden games. Maybe even a swimming pool. We were drifting along, in a bit of a daze actually what with having been up half the night and then very early again in the morning, me in a long, floaty dress and him in a very tight tee shirt which showed his tattoos (Leeds United and a yin-yang symbol; he was a complicated boy) when suddenly, there was a snarling noise and two toothy dogs leapt out of the grass and started barking and leaping up at us. I screamed.

"Fini!" shouted a voice, and the two dogs reluctantly subsided. Now we saw a short, upright old Frenchman in a tweed coat (in this weather!) emerging from behind a tree. He came towards us, scowling in an entirely unfriendly manner. Now we noticed that he carried a shotgun over his shoulder.

"What," he enquired in French with a very strong provencal accent, "are you doing on my land?"

I replied, also in French, but with very strong English accent, that I was looking at the house and that I understood that the land belonged to the house.

"Non, non, non!" he shouted, and the dogs looked up, clearly hoping that they might be allowed to bite us after all. "The land is mine. This house has NO land, you understand?"

"Er -" (French or English).

"NO land!"

"I understand. But I thought - ?"

"You are?"

"I'm - er - from England. I was thinking I might..." Oh, what was the use? "Who are you, anyway?"

"I am the neighbour. I own all this land -" and he waved his arm to encompass everything between here and the horizon, lavender fields, mountains, trees, river, and some tiny distant figures shooting something - possibly English tourists -

"You're really thinking of buying this house?"

I said yes I was. The man looked contemptuous, in that very French way, wrinkling up his nose as if he could smell something bad. Maybe he could.

"This is your son?" he enquired, looking Jimmy up and down.

"No, he's my friend. He's a builder," I added, defensively.

"Ha!" he said, and whether that was French or English I couldn't be sure.

"Go to the mairie. Go! See! The mayor has the plans of all the houses in the village. He will show you, on the plan, what land belongs to what house. It will be clear, even to you, English woman. See the plans. If you don't believe me. Au revoir, madame. Monsieur."

He strode off, whistling to the dogs to follow him, which they did slinking along with many a backward glance of disappointment. We retreated and went round to the front of the house to stand on the drive and await the agent. I was a bit shaken and Jimmy comforted me. In fact he was just in the middle of a very effective bit of comforting when there was a mighty roaring noise and the agent arrived in his shiny new car.

"Bonjour, bonjour," he warbled, kissing me four times and shaking Jimmy's hand. I explained that Jimmy was an English builder and he was going to advise me.

"I assure you it is entirely unnecessary, all the works in the house are new and it has been most carefully renovated," Patreek said, and I translated.

"We'll see," Jimmy said, and as his tone of voice spoke for itself I didn't bother to translate.

We walked round the house and the agent said quite a lot, which I translated, and Jimmy said very little, but looked grave.

"Damp," he remarked in the cellar. "Possible subsidence. Look at those cracks in the walls."

In the barn, "roof." Was all he said.

"Window frame," he said in bedroom one.

"It's the original window," said Patreek, picking this up and replying somewhat defensively. "It has been well maintained."

"Oh yeah, maybe for a bit," said Jimmy, poking at the central upright wooden bar, part of which which crumbled beneath his touch, "but it's been a bit neglected recently."

"Er - negligee," I translated uncertainly. Maybe I was crazed with lust and couldn't stop thinking of sexy words.

The agent looked puzzled. "Negligee?"

"La fenêtre," I said helpfully. In a haze of misunderstanding we went through the rest of the house.

"You can't buy this house," Jimmy said. "There are too many problems. And you have to find out about the land. We need to do some more research. And even if you had the land, it would cost a packet to fix this little lot. Do you have that much money?"

We went outside, and I whispered to Jimmy that we would go back to the B and B and reconsider. Now the agent revealed his trump card. His car was blocking ours in.

"So, now you come to the office to sign the papers? I have the notaire ready, he will be more expensive if we keep him waiting," he laughed, showing all his teeth, like the dogs, "never keep a lawyer waiting, ha ha!"

"I'm afraid we're going to have to keep him waiting," I said firmly, while trembling with anxiety, "as I have to go back to the guest house to collect some things. I also need to see the mayor."

"But why?"

"I met the neighbour."

"Ah. I see. You have been talking to the neighbour. The neighbour, you know, is a great liar." Patreek was visibly shaking with rage. "He is famous in this area for his lies. I hope you haven't been listening to him?"

"I expect you're right," I said politely, "however I need to go and check some things, also some complicated bank and money things," I improvised, "before I sign anything."

"You are making a big mistake," Patreek said. I was extremely glad that Jimmy, with all his tattoos, was right there.

"Well, even so." I said. "Banks and money," I said firmly.

There was a pause. He had to move his car to let us go.

"You must ring me in less than one hour," he said eventually, through gritted teeth.

"Alright, I will."

"Very well." Reluctantly he got into his car and backed it out of the way. I revved up and sped off, rather churning up the track in the process, and changing gear with no difficulty at all.

The mayor, on the other hand, was charm and delightfulness itself, but also spoke no English.

"The neighbour is quite right," he said, "the house has no land, apart from a small area at the front, the other area has been used by the house owners in the past, as a benefit to them. The owners live abroad and only visit the house occasionally so it was not a problem."

He showed me the map, which he kept in his office.

"You see here, the outline in red? But since they objected to the neighbour's planning permission, the gloves are off and it is war. He doesn't give permission for anything any more. He owns all the land right around the house, including the access road. He is the biggest land owner in the village. And you know he breeds hunting dogs?"

"Mmm, yes, we met some of them."

"A very important man."

"Important not to offend him?"

"I think you are an intelligent lady."

"Well, we understand each other."

"Yes, we do."

Jimmy was looking a bit annoyed, as I had not been translating. Actually the mayor had reminded me of my early call centre life, it was even possible that in those seemingly fardistant days I had rung him up and pestered him about printers.

As we left, Jimmy said, " He fancied you, you know."

"Really?" I said. "I never noticed."

"Well I think the way he kissed your hand was a bit of a give away."

"That's just being French," I laughed.

"Just being French!" Jimmy spluttered, "so French is just another word for creepy bastard now?"

We were on the verge of another sexy row, and I knew where that would lead, but first I had to ring Patreek, the lying creepy French bastard.

"I think you have not told me the truth," I told him. This made him cross.

"I never rolled anyone in the flour," he riposted. This was too French for me.

"Look," I said, "I'm not buying the house. It's like this. Too many problems. Too little land."

"I never realised the English were so dishonourable," the oily maggot had the nerve to reply.

"I never realised the French were capable of being so truthful," I replied, turning claret with rage, "your mayor was a revelation."

And with that, I rang off. And Jimmy and I had our sexy row, to which we had been building up, and our even sexier reconciliation, over and after dinner with truffles. And snails. And oysters.

But clearly, this kind of thing was unsustainable, and shortly after we returned to Blighty, we agreed that, enjoyable though it had been, we should stop dallying with one another. It was wonderfully civilised, and ensured that we could work together in the future without rancour or bitterness. Once again, I marvelled at the capacity of the young to keep it simple. But I still felt terrible.

Chapter 14

Lady Chalk of Billingsgate

The worst thing was, there was no-one I could talk to about this self-loathing. Carla was gone, my friends from the village, Ian and Maggie, were away on holiday, Naz and Jen would have spread it all round the office so I couldn't tell them, also they would just laugh, couldn't tell mum, and Jane - Jane would have to do.

"Hi Jane, can you talk?"

"As it happens I was just sitting with my feet up for ten minutes until I have to fetch Seb from swimming. I'm having a cup of tea and a ginger nut."

"Are you dunking?"

"I am indeed."

Sometimes, just occasionally, Jane was the perfect sister.

"I need to confess to someone. You're the only person I can talk to."

"That seems to be my role. Only this week I had a patient, a ten year old boy who told me exactly how he wanted to kill his mother in carefully thought out detail. Clearly he had been longing to tell someone."

"Gosh, how was he going to do it?"

"Well, it started with razor blades. It was a slow process."

"I don't think I need to hear any more."

"I think he has a future as a film director."

"If only he were Spanish."

"Mmmm. So what do you need to confess?"

"Apart from how I'd kill Mother? I thought bilberry jam with just a few deadly nightshade berries in there might do it. Or redcurrant and yew."

"A thoughtful, home-made gift, how delightful. You could put a bow round it as a finishing touch. And a handwritten label, only you would disguise the handwriting, of course."

"But that isn't why I rang."

"So?"

"Well - it's awful - I've been sleeping around and I feel terrible."

"Have you been tested?"

"I don't mean that kind of terrible, and anyway there were condoms involved, since you care. But I am a bit itchy, now you mention it. Oh, hell."

"I'm glad you're at least being semi-responsible," Jane said sternly. "Condoms, I mean. How do you feel terrible? Apart from itchy?"

"I suppose I feel like a slut."

"Maybe you are a slut?"

"I'm not!"

"Define slut."

"No, you define slut."

"Someone who sleeps around with men she's not in love with."

"You're not being very understanding," I said. I wanted to cry. Sometimes, Jane was the nastiest sister in the world.

"Do you think I'm a slut, then?"

"Yes, I do. And I think you should examine your priorities. What about your family? What about Nancy?"

"She's at her dad's," I mumbled.

"I think you're falling apart, Holly," Jane said with the unmistakeable triumphant note of the righteous married person, "you probably need help. Now, I must go and pick up my son. Bye. Take care now. Look after yourself."

And she rang off.

Now I felt worse than ever. Maybe Jane was right and I needed help. I looked at myself in the mirror. My hair was fine, these days, thanks to expert intervention, but there a funny look in the eyes, and the mouth was distinctly disappointed. In fact, I was starting to look like my mother. I had to pull myself together, quickly. But how? The phone rang, as I stared sadly at my image. It was Jimmy.

"Hey - guess what? - I've got thrush," he said in his direct, I'm-a-young-person way.

"Oh? Ugh. I'm sorry to hear it. And?"

"Well. You should get tested or summink."

"Oh, of course. Okay. I will. Cheers, Jimmy. Everything ok with you? Apart from that?"

"Yeah, sweet."

"Super."

"We should go out together again some time, it was well good."

Why is he talking like that? I blame the media.

"Yes, Jimmy, we must think about something we could - er - see at the pictures or - er but I have to go now."

Thrush? Oh God. A sexually transmitted disease. God's minimum punishment for promiscuity. Was this proof of the existence of God? I didn't like to think that, if God existed, he would be so petty. It would make me think less of Him. Not that I'd ever thought much about Him. Maybe this was where I had gone wrong. After all, marriage vows are about religion, aren't they? I was married in church. Maybe I had sinned by not sticking with the man I had vowed, in what now seemed to me a fairly ridiculous farrago of superstitious claptrap, to love forever.

The phone rang again. It was Nancy.

"Just to let you know, mum, dad's being really supportive and all -"

CHAPTER 14. LADY CHALK OF BILLINGSGATE

"Does he know about the horrible teacher?"

"Yes, and he's being really understanding and not stressing out like you do -"

"Understanding?" I said incredulously.

"Yes, and I'm going to stay here. For a while. I can't say how long. See you, mum."

"But -"

But she was gone. Oh, God was really rubbing it in, now, wasn't He? What would be next? As a precaution I turned the telephone off at the wall. Then I had a bit of a cry. Then I looked at myself in the mirror again, and, unsurprisingly, I looked worse than ever. I spoke to the tragic woman in the mirror.

"What are you going to do?" I asked her. "Look at you. You're a mess, you have no house, no daughter who loves you, no husband, no boyfriend, no proper job, no proper friends, no plan for the future, no self-esteem, no social life, no purpose to your existence - and you're talking to yourself."

I stopped. The woman had suffered enough. I should tell her something nice. "On the other hand," I said, "your hair looks okay."

I paused.

"And you have your health, as far as we know, apart from a spot of thrush, and some money." I added. "Now, what I want you to do is to draw up a plan for the future, based on that list you did for Nancy, when she still loved you. I am going to be your counsellor. Your life coach. Now pull yourself together and get on with it."

Two hours later I had not made much progress, apart from deciding to ask Basil if he knew anyone who could give me a proper job. One that I would like doing. But at least I was thinking about a future. I had decided that what I needed was a makeover in the Last Chance Salon.

Just before I went to bed that night, I remembered that I'd turned the phone off, so I switched it back on. There was a message.

"Olly? This is Martine. I have been trying to contact you. I know I said I would never speak to you again, 'owever, it is urgent. It is a police matter. There is unfortunately someone who keeps ringing the office and trying to find out your address. We told him we couldn't help him, of course, and warned him that he must stop, we also explained that you do not, and will never again, work in this building, but he has now been to the office in person and the receptionist felt that his manner was threatening ("sreatening") so we have ad no choice but to inform the police. I'm sorry to say you are being stalked. Please contact me if you require further information. Sank you."

Chapter 15

I have the painters in

I decided to ignore Martine. A stalker indeed. Unless it was that French estate agent... but no, Martine would have loved him, not reported him to the police. Now I thought about it, they were so horrid they could have been related. The first thing I did was to get down to the chemist's and bought myself a surprisingly expensive cure for thrush. Who would have guessed that it would cost twelve pounds? As a punishment, presumably.

I rang Anders, and rather smugly informed him that I had thrush, and that he should look out for symptoms. Anders flew into a bit of a panic, presumably confusing thrush with nastier things like herpes and AIDS, but I couldn't be bothered to explain the difference to him, and simply referred him to an English/Swedish dictionary. I also went to the doctor and made an appointment to be tested for all other known sexually transmitted diseases, just to be on the safe side. Whether it was the medication, the rummaging about that was apparently necessary in order to check me out for genital fungi and viruses, or the early onset of menopause, I don't know, but I had the most massive period I had ever had, ever. It was actually quite cathartic, as if I was bleeding all my former life away. It was also entirely inconvenient as I was back at work and the call centre rule was that you could only go to the toilet twice in any session, not including breaks. I had to go every half hour or, even with extra absorbent super strength protection the room would soon have looked like the scene of a particularly gruesome massacre. My frequent absences soon attracted the wrath of the supervisor.

"What the hell's the matter with you?" he demanded. "Bad night on the curry and lager? I didn't think you were the type?"

"I'm not - that is to say, I like curry and lager, but that's not the problem on this occasion. It's women's problems," I added primly.

"Oh, bloody Mr Blobby," he said, stomping back to desk in disgust, "It'd better not go on tomorrow, or you'll be out on your ear."

"It won't." I hoped it wouldn't.

Luckily it was a lot better the next day, but it left me afraid that the one thing I had going for me, apart from the new improved hair, in other words my formerly robust health, was about to let me down. That would be awful, because then I'd only have the hair, and frankly that was all the work of my fabulous new hairdresser, and if I were to find myself, say, shipwrecked on a desert island, it would quickly revert to its natural state of frightfulness. Then I would have nothing going for me at all. On the other hand, it would give me a whole new set of challenges which would probably drive my present anxieties entirely out of my mind. Hmm, maybe I should set sail in a small and unsuitable craft. But no, I remembered the horror voyage with Roger and decided not to risk it. Thus I mused as I drove to see Basil. I had made an appointment, on the grounds that he was the only person who still liked me, so even if I had to pay to see him, it would be worth it.

He ushered me into his office as formerly, and we beamed at each other across our cups of tea like Mrs Tittlemouse and Mr Jackson. (I was taking the role of Mr Jackson).

"It's always delightful to see you, Holly, but I'm not sure what I can do for you?"

"Carla's still missing, I still haven't addressed the paedophile teacher question, oh and there's a new one now: I'm being stalked."

"Stalked?"

I explained.

"This does sound potentially serious. Did you say the police are involved?" I had only thrown this in to make it sound as if I had a proper legal problem. Really I was only making excuses to see Basil and building up to asking him if he could help me to find a job.

"Well - er - I don't think it's all that important - just the call centre making a mountain out of a molehill..."

"Don't worry, Holly, I'll get to the bottom of it. Leave it with me."

"Okay - er -"

"The other things are as before. I suggest you try to get some evidence that this teacher is preying on other young girls if you want to have any kind of case against him."

"Oh, well."

"I know you're disappointed, but these cases are particularly difficult. Nancy is sixteen and refusing to make a statement."

"But his professional conduct -"

"That's the only angle to take. Now, this stalker business is something else." Basil was back in knight in shining armour mode. "I'm going to find out what's going on."

While I sipped my tea, Basil rang the police and had a conversation during which he wrote a lot of things down. I didn't listen much. I knew it was all Martine getting her French knickers in a twist. When he got off the phone, Basil turned to me and looked at me over his glasses. I expect I look better that way.

"The police haven't followed it up yet. The name that the man has given, the police think is an alias."

"What is it?"

Basil consulted his notes.

"Steve Harley, apparently the name of some sort of rock singer?"

"Oh my God!" I knocked my teacup over as I sat up. Luckily it was empty.

"As I said, the police think it's not his real name."

"No, I know him!"

"You know a rock singer?"

"No, no, I know Steve - it's not the real Steve Harley -"

"That's what the police seem to think."

"Oh gosh, this is getting confusing. Do the police have any contact details?"

"I don't know," Basil said. "But if this man is a threat to you, why would you -?"

"He's not, he's an old school friend, I talked to him on the phone when I was working at the call centre. Oh, God, he must have been trying to get in touch with me all this time!"

"So you want to talk to him?"

"Yes! Of course I do!"

Basil looked at me in a bemused way but kindly rang the police again, and got me a phone number. He wrote it down for me on a piece of paper. I held it in my hand as if it was an unexploded bomb.

"Shall I ring him for you? The police are not convinced that you should contact this man."

"No, no, I'll do it later." I said hastily. "But Basil, what I really, really need is a new job I hate working in call centres, it's draining my life away. I wondered if you had any jobs going here? Or if you know anybody who could employ me?"

Basil looked at me over his specs again. He pursed his lips thoughtfully.

"I'll see what I can do," he said.

I went home with the piece of paper with Steve's number on it. I noticed that the hand that held it, was shaking. Good job I wasn't in bomb disposal. I sat at the dining table, looking at the paper with numbers on it. I'd ring him later. When I'd decided what to say. Two days later, when Basil rang me late in the evening, the piece of paper was still on the table, though I had picked it up a couple of times. Yeah - right, a couple of times a minute.

"Good news, Holly - I think I've got you a job!"

"Really?"

"Friend of mine runs a small business," Basil said a bit vaguely, "was saying the other night that he could do with a bit of a hand in the office. Would that be the ticket?"

"What kind of small business?" I not unreasonably asked.

"Do you know, I'm not entirely sure. Import export type of thing, I think. Excellent chap, though, won't give you any bother, salt of the earth. Give him a ring tomorrow and mention my name. His name is Figgy - not sure what his real name is, suppose that's a nickname."

"But I can't ask for Figgy."

"Suppose he must have another name. Hang on a tick, the wife might know." I could hear him shouting "Maud! What's Figgy's name? Can't have her asking for Figgy! Has he got a real name? Oh."

Back on the line, Basil said, "Figgy's name is Lionel, apparently, God knows how Lionel turned into Figgy. Never heard him called anything but Figgy, but you'd better ask for Lionel."

"Alright then, I will, thanks Basil."

"Let me know how you get on."

"Bye then."

Basil seemed reluctant to hang up the phone and there was a bit of heavy breathing at his end which seemed to indicate that he had something else to add.

"Was that it?"

"Er - just - Figgy - he, well. Oh, you'll see. Goodbye then, Holly."

So now I had two phone calls which I was reluctant to make. Calling Steve suddenly seemed like the easy option, compared to the enigmatic Figgy. Hastily and without further, potentially alarming thought I dialled the number.

"Hello," said the voice.

"Hello, this is the Aston Martin helpline," I said.

"Holly!"

"Hi."

Gosh, what did we say now?

"I've been trying to get hold of you," he said.

"I kept being told I had a stalker," I explained.

"I suppose it did look a bit sinister."

"But you finally got through."

"And we won't get cut off this time?"

"Not if I can help it."

"I'd really like to meet up, Holly. Can we arrange something? I'd rather talk to you face to face. Let's have a drink, or a meal, or something."

"Alright then. I'll have a shandy with you. Do you remember - that time -?"

"Let's not talk now. I want to save everything for when you're there."

"OK then. Can you get over this way?"

We arranged to meet up. It was most peculiar. I had a sense of everything having been planned already. I rang off with a feeling of profound contentment, as if I was swimming calmly in a deep and peaceful sea towards a distant, scented, tropical shore. Then I went to bed. I slept profoundly for the first time since I had been run away from. I slept right through the night, and was shocked to see that it was seven o'clock when I woke up, and not 3.37 as it usually was. (I had become distressingly familiar with the night time schedule of the World Service, which I can, from experience, heartily recommend for its soporific effect)

I had been having a dream which I was convinced was important, though at first the details were vague.

As I drove in to work, I recalled the dream. I had been in a house which was somewhere I used to live. It was empty, and I was looking around. I was surprised to find that there was another wing on the house, where I had never been before, and which seemed to be in need of some repair. Wandering around the wing, I met a man ironing curtains. What was that about?

Work that day was so particularly dreary and dismal that I finally resolved to ring Figgy. Anything had to be better than this. At lunchtime I got out my new mobile and fiddled with its buttons. Jimmy saw me and came over to show me how to use it.

"You OK?"

"Of course. Are you?"

"Hey, missing you."

"Well, that's nice, I'm flattered, but I'm dating someone else now," I lied. Well. It was only half a lie, as I had arranged to meet Steve.

"Are you ringing him now?"

"Oh, no no no, I'm ringing a man about a job."

"Really. I'll leave you in peace, then."

"Ta."

"Oh - did the you-know-what clear up?"

"The what?"

"You know. Lady Chalk of Billingsgate."

"What are you on about?"

"Thrush," I hissed.

"Oh, yes, of course. Just stuck me dick in some yogurt."

"Brilliant."

"See you around, then."

Jimmy retreated. I was suddenly sorry for him. He was young and tough. And it had been his idea that we shouldn't carry on. It had been all his doing. But he was sweet. So. Anyway. Why did I always feel guilty?

"Hello, is this Fig - I mean, Lionel?"

"Yes," he barked. "Who is this?"

"Basil - my solicitor - told me to call you about a job."

"Ah! Yes! Basil's girl. Spoke very highly of you. I was telling him, I need a factotum."

"A whatotum?"

"Can you do everything?"

"I suppose so - it sort of depends what everything encompasses."

"Computers, invoices, make the tea and wipe my arse kind of thing?"

"Yes to the first three. I assume the last one was metaphorical?"

"Ha ha ha ha," roared Figgy. "Start tomorrow. I like a girl with a bit of pluck."

"A bit of - ?" I was enquiring but he had gone.

CHAPTER 15. I HAVE THE PAINTERS IN

It occurred to me that I didn't know where to go, so I rang back, and gathered that he was very close by, in Morton Spa, on a small industrial estate, just off the main road.

In fact it was so close that I could have walked to work, but as I wasn't sure I had cycled. I parked my bike behind the premises, and walked round to the front of the building, which I now saw had a sign which proclaimed Ooh You Saucepot. Hoping against hope that this meant that Figgy dealt in fine crockery and esoteric cooking utensils I went in, only to be slapped round the face by a rubber miniskirt which was flapping excitedly in the breeze from the open door. Disentangling myself from its gluey embrace I went tentatively forward into the rather gloomy depths. There was no-one around, but a sign pointed to "Office" so that was the direction I took.

Soon I noticed a door with "Lionel Lamb, Managing Director" written on it, and was about to knock when I realised he was on the phone. I didn't want to interrupt. "No, really, old chap, that's a terrible idea, don't think for a moment I can do it at that price. Got to have some kind of tiny profit margin this end, you know. Not a bloody charitable organisation. What? - thing is, old boy, need to keep body and soul together. It's dog eats dog. No, I'm not criticising you chaps for eating dog. Can we stick to the point? What you eat is your business. I'm doing you a favour, old pal. Well haven't I taken them all before? If I increase the order I expect you to do them cheaper, that's the way it works. I know you've all been labouring under the yoke of communism and you don't really cotton on yet, but - what? - well, is there anyone there who speaks English? Thing is, dear boy, it's my best offer. Twenty-five pence each, and I'll take twenty thousand. Can't say fairer. Next week it'll be twenty pence. Take it or leave it."

He seemed to have hung up, so I knocked and went in. Figgy almost fell over in his haste to stand up for a lady. As it was he knocked his chair over.

"My goodness," he spluttered, "and to what do I owe the honour?"

He was, as I had already surmised from his voice and manner, a large, red-faced tweedy man in his late fifties.

"I'm Holly Field," I said.

"Aha! Basil's young lady!"

"Not so much of the young," I protested. "Or the lady, for that matter," I added.

"Splendid, wonderful, just what the doctor ordered," he said, rubbing his hands together.

I felt as if I had wandered onto the set of Carry on Doing Your Naughty Business.

"I might get you to wear some of the merchandise, later on," he added, looking me up and down. Now, how had I known that he was going to say that?

"It's good for the customers to see it in action, so to speak."

So why wasn't he in a leather thong, I refrained from enquiring. Maybe he was. Under his tweeds. What a very alarming thought. I tried not to think it. Figgy gave me a tour of the premises, which were awash with saucy items, and showed me what he wanted me to do, which was fortunately entirely innocuous and consisted of the usual answering the phone, dealing with petty cash and invoices, and filing. I settled in straightaway and familiarised myself with the setup. There were few other staff, apart from van drivers who arrived and departed very regularly, thrusting grubby pieces of paper at me as they did so.

Figgy now wandered off for his lunch as it was ten thirty. I was to learn that Figgy was the last of the Great British Lunchers. He returned at three, smelling as if he had fallen into a butt of Malmsey, or possibly of Black Sheep, and spent the afternoon dozing peacefully at his desk, occasionally waking up to answer a phone call. It was a good job, as I was able to get on with things in my own way, had the satisfaction of finishing a great many small tasks, and had immense interest in the merchandise and the customers. Figgy's catalogue was a revelation. I realised what a hitherto sheltered life I had led. Why had I never felt a need to acquire any of this stuff? Why did I still not? (Though I did rather like some of the underwear. And there was a nice leather jacket...) I had some lovely chats with people ordering items for their shops, taking over the role of sales person when Figgy was absent. Figgy was pleased with me.

"Excellent work, Holly," he said one day, "so pleased that you've taken to the world of adult toys. Any time you want to take something home with you, you just let me know, and I'll do you a discount," and he winked mightily.

"Do you have a shop of your own?" I asked, to deflect the conversation.

"I have three, at present," Figgy replied, "but I intend to open a couple more when I find the right premises. That's what I do all day, you know," he went on, as if this excuse had just occurred to him, "I drive around looking for premises."

I sincerely hoped he wasn't driving anywhere. I liked Figgy. It was easy to get very fond of him, he was such a poppet. I gathered that his wife had left him a number of years ago. He lived alone, but apparently had a great many "lady friends" to console him. He seemed to have a heart of gold, but possibly this was yet another example of my inability to spot a charlatan masquerading as a nice person. Nevertheless, I soon settled into my working life at Ooh You Saucepot and Figgy and I had many a jolly pre-lunch chat. After lunch he was, he explained, always too tired to talk much. It was to do with his metabolism, which slowed down while he was digesting, he said.

My life at home settled down, too. I was used to the absence of Nancy, though it still hurt. While we were still waiting for her exam results, no decisions had to be made about schools. Maybe she would live with her dad. Then I could go anywhere. Well. Fancy that.

I told Figgy about Nancy one morning, and he was suitably shocked. In spite of his tawdry trade in strap-on dildoes and rubber aprons, he had the moral outrage of religious fundamentalist. Never before had I seen someone literally spluttering with indignation. Of course, Figgy was a natural splutterer anyway.

"He should be struck off! They can't let people like that loose in schools! Have you contacted the newspapers?"

"I'm sort of planning to go through the proper channels," I said, "but as school's closed at the moment it's a bit tricky."

"Give me the name of the little toerag," Figgy said.

"What are you going to do?" I asked, alarmed.

"Just ask some friends for information."

"Well if you promise not to do anything rash... it's Graeme Birch."

"I'll make some enquiries," said Figgy, darkly. I hoped it wasn't going to be wire brushing, again. Maybe it would be something more exotic and even more unpleasant involving adult equipment from the darker and more sinister end of the catalogue.

But all this was driven from my mind by the prospect of my date with Steve, which loomed. I wanted to call it off, I was so terrified. Why? Well, for a start, I realised as I gave some thought to the question, Steve was one of the best things from my childhood. The times I'd spent with him had been some of the happiest I could remember. What if I had to shatter all those memories because he turned out to be a creep? (He hadn't sounded like a creep on the phone). I would have lost something I could never get back. Even if it was an illusion. I felt like Proust, about to sink his teeth into the madeleine, only with terrible foreknowledge of what was to come. I desperately wanted to see Steve, but at the same time, I desperately didn't. We had arranged to meet at a pub which did really good food, out in the Dales. Steve had read about it in a guide to the best pubs in England, he said. He was going to stay the night there , so that he didn't have to drive home. I was a bit concerned about this, hoping that there wasn't an assumption in his mind about where I would spend the night. At least he hadn't expected me to put him up. Also I was quite impressed, in spite of berating myself for shallowness, that he had such good taste and could afford to indulge it.

My usual nerves about the right clothes to wear overcame me and I had no lovely Nancy to advise me, so I went to a terrifyingly posh shop in Morton Spa which was advertising its summer sale

(70% off, so maybe I could just afford the clothes) and asked the assistant if she had an outfit which said "I normally wear this sort of clothes, but I'm not posh, I just have naturally good taste, and I'm really relaxed." She pointed out that this was a bit of a tall order, particularly in view of my challenging figure (cheek!) but an hour and a half later I emerged into the sunshine with a posh cloth bag containing a very expensive dress (floral silk chiffon) and a cardigan that looked like a jacket. Or was it a jacket that looked like a cardigan? Now all I had to do was to go on the date. Oh dear.

I have never been so nervous in my life as I was driving to the pub and parking my car. My hand shook as I locked the doors. At least I knew I looked fabulous. I walked up to the front door with the confidence that came from knowing that everything, from hair to shoes, was perfect. I strode into the bar, and people turned to look. The women frowned, and looked me up and down. That proved it. I was right, I looked fantastic. I walked all around the room and came back to the point where I had started, by the door. But there was no-one in the bar who could possible be Steve. At least I hoped not. I took out my phone to check the time and realised that I was slightly early. Then I noticed that I had a text message. It was from Nancy.

"On way home pls collect station 8.07 c u N xxx"

I went outside again and stood in the evening sunshine in the tiny front garden so as not to disturb the other customers with my vulgar mobile phoning.

"What's going on? Where are you? Of course, I'm delighted that you're coming back, but -"

"But? What do you mean but? It's me - your only daughter - remember?" The egocentricity of the young.

"I'm on a date."

"I see, and that's more important than your daughter is it?"

"No, it's just that I'm out in the country, miles away, I'm nor sure if I can get to the station in time."

"I'm on the train now."

"Why have you left?"

"Oh, you know, I just got fed up. It's a bit boring here."

I became aware out of the corner of my eye of a tall man approaching the pub. I backed into some bushes. He hesitated as he saw me, then went in. I pretended not to have noticed him.

"Look, Nancy," I said, "I'll ring you again in five minutes and tell you what I'm going to do. Alright?"

"It'll have to be, won't it?"

I dragged myself out of the bushes again, unfortunately snagging my expensive cardigan/jacket in the process. I went back into the pub, looking slightly less perfect than formerly. My heels had sunk into the ground and were covered in mud, I had cobweb or something similar all over the skirt of my dress, and I had a small slug on my leg, I noticed as I glanced down. Curses. The tall man I had noticed earlier came over and kissed my cheek.

"I knew it was you, hiding from me in the hedge," he said. "You haven't changed a bit."

"You've grown," I said.

"I know, my mum thought I would never stop. I cost her a fortune in socks, she tells me."

There was a rather peculiar smell near Steve but I decided to ignore it. He was gorgeous, apart from the smell. He was one of the happiest people I had ever met. We made our way to the bar, got some drinks and started to reminisce.

"The raft we made that time - and it sank half way across just where it was actually deep - and your sister was on it -"

"Yeah I was in a lot of trouble over that one."

"I still say it was a good raft. I think she must have sabotaged it."

"It would have been typical."

Then I suddenly remembered Nancy.

"I have to pick up my daughter!"

"I'll come with you."

"Oh."

"If you don't mind. Come on, let's go!"

"Okay, then," I said, somewhat bemused. I was the bossy one who told people what to do. What was going on?

The peculiar smell followed us out of the pub and Steve kindly informed me that I had cat poo on my shoe.

"When did you notice?" I asked, frantically wiping it off on the grass before I got in the car.

"Oh, straight away," he said, "I thought you were refreshingly scruffy."

"Thanks."

"That's quite alright. Now, hop in."

"Let's go in mine," I suggested, "in case there's any more cat poo on my person."

The car he had been about to let me into, while still not an Aston Martin, was rather beautiful, and I didn't feel quite smart enough for it. I led him across the car park to my rather battered but beloved Volvo, and while I drove through the narrow windy lanes between dry stone walls in the fading golden light, Steve shuffled through my CD collection, occasionally snorting with laughter.

"What - what? What's so funny?"

"You haven't half got some rubbish."

"In your opinion."

In this amicable way we arrived at the station and I realised that I hadn't told Nancy that I would have someone else with me.

"Stay in the car," I said hastily.

"OK," he said, "in that case can I listen to Madonna?"

"Hmmm," I said, but really I liked this teasing.

I hastened into the station and found my daughter. She was sitting curled up on a bench, reading.

"Hello, darling." I buried my face in her neck and smelled her familiar smell.

"Mum, I missed you," she said, snuffling slightly. We both snuffled slightly.

"Um," I said, "okay, listen. There's someone in the car. My date."

"Oh."

"You'll like him," I said, "anyway he's not a proper date, he's an old school friend."

"Off the internet?" she asked scornfully.

"As it happens, no. It's a long story and I'll tell it to you some time. But not now. Here he is. Steve, this is my daughter, Nancy."

"Hello, Nancy. It's very nice to meet you." He held out his hand, and, very reluctantly, Nancy shook it.

"Hello."

"Do you want to come and eat with us, Nancy?" Steve asked her.

"No, thanks, I just want to go home and crash. If that's ok with you."

"That's fine," I interrupted hastily, "Steve and I will go and eat and I'll see you later."

We dropped her off at home after a silent journey from the station. When we were alone again, Steve said: "That's one unhappy young woman."

"I know," I said, "it's so hard to know what to do for the best."

I told him about the teacher and how she had got so angry with me.

"You need some evidence to show her that this guy is just a slime ball," he said. "I'll help you. But let's talk about that later. Just for now, let's stick with the happy stuff. Let's go back to talking about when we were eleven. I was really enjoying that."

"Me too," I assured him.

We had a wonderful meal but I barely noticed what I was eating. Between the pudding and the coffee he took my hand and turned it over.

"This is brilliant, Holly," he said.

"I know."

"Will you come to my room with me - just for half an hour - I want to hold you. That's all. Just for now."

"Yes."

We went to his room. He held me. It was all. It was brilliant. After the shortest half hour of my life, I went home to Nancy.

CHAPTER 15. I HAVE THE PAINTERS IN

"Oh, mum, it's awful, dad has this horrible girlfriend called Mimi."

"Oh, I see."

"She's a cow. She was being a cow, so I had to tell her what a cow she was. Dad said I couldn't talk to her like that. I said she couldn't talk to me like that. He said she could. So I left."

"Fair enough. But I must warn you, I think I may have this horrible boyfriend called Steve."

"No, it's alright, Steve's cool. But that Mimi - mum, I don't think I can ever go back there. She's such a cow. She told me I couldn't have wine, and she made me do the washing up, and she used my perfume without asking, and she was just horrible! I can't understand why dad puts up with her for a second!"

"I expect things will pan out. If we let them. Maybe he'll go off her."

It was lovely to go to sleep knowing that my baby was back in her room, zizzing peacefully among the crumpled towels, abandoned cups of tea, stubs of eyeliner and assorted cuddly toys which made up her world.

I saw Steve briefly before I went to work and he went home.

"Have you got any idea what I went through to get in touch with you again?"

"Don't exaggerate."

"I was interviewed by the police. My neighbours still lock their car doors every time they drive off. They haven't asked me to look after the cat when they're on holiday, either."

"Every cloud has a silver lining."

"I never felt like this before," he said.

I had the usual horrible feeling he would never call me.

Chapter 16

Of Imperial Barges and Chinese tools

Figgy was in a buoyant mood the next day and spent a joyous hour on the phone to his suppliers getting giant penises at rock bottom prices. When he was on form he was a giant among negotiators, but unfortunately it was lunchtime all too soon and after that Figgy was deflated and fit for nothing. I spent the day sorting out the petty cash, which was in turmoil thanks to Figgy's habit of saying, for example, that he was taking ten pounds when he was actually taking twenty. When I berated him for this habit, he explained that there was no point in putting twenty as he only expected to spend ten. The other ten was " - to be on the safe side. And I almost always put the rest back, so you see, it would be silly to put twenty."

"You can amend the amount when you get back," I pointed out.

"Feminine logic, dear girl," Figgy said patronisingly, "this is why men rule the world, I think you'll find. We don't generate paperwork the way you ladies do. We keep it simple."

Only because you leave your mess for other people to clear up, I thought crossly.

"Now you'll be pleased with me," Figgy went on.

"Really?" I replied, failing to keep all the sarcasm out of my voice.

"Now, now," said sensitive Figgy, "I've been doing research on your behalf. That teacher fella, the one who should be castrated and hung in chains from the castle walls as an example to all."

"Oh, yes?"

"Found a chap who knows him. Says he's basically a decent bloke, which I find hard to believe. Weak, fella says. Fallible."

"You didn't tell him about Nancy?"

"Course not, what do you take me for? No, I simply made inquiries. I said someone had recommended him as a tutor for my niece and I needed to know if he was a sound chap."

"That was a good story."

"I was quite chuffed with it," said Figgy modestly. "Anyway, it turns out that he goes to two different pubs, one when he's out with the lads, which is evidently not all that often, not really a man's man. That type."

"I can imagine."

"Then there's this other watering hole where he goes with the little ladies."

"Oh please!"

"Sorry. Any which way, the chap said we could catch him in either of those places to chat about tutoring, as he didn't have a phone number. I suggest we stake it out and take some photos, what about it?"

"I think that's brilliant!"

"I told you you'd be pleased with me," he said as he toddled off to lunch with a twenty pound note.

Because he was such a super sleuth, I ran the Carla scenario past Figgy the next morning. "I do know an enormous number of people, I'm sure one of my pals will know her. African connection, you say? Rings a bell, as it happens. I don't mind betting that Mungo's run across her. He has African connections. It's a while since I sank a couple with Mungo, probably about time I did. Leave it with me."

Steve rang me at eleven.

"Has he gone? Can I ring you at work?"

"Yes and yes. He wouldn't mind even if he was here. He's the model employer, apart from a couple of minor peccadilloes, or peckerdildoes as Figgy would say. What are you doing?"

"Just arsing about in the office. I had to cancel a meeting, and I thought, what task would I like to prioritise?"

"How sweet. What exactly do you do in your office?"

"Oh God, I don't know. I go to meetings and fall asleep."

"I don't understand what your job is at all."

"That makes two of us. I just keep my head down and hope no-one finds out that I don't know anything."

"What do you say in meetings?"

"I go on about business processes and try to use obscure phrases that no-one fully understands. I mean, for God's sake, what's - to take at random an example from a document on my desk - synchronized productivity creation? - whatever it is, you can be sure I'll be saying it at my next meeting."

"Does no-one ever ask what things mean?"

"No, because they're afraid of looking stupid. The thing is to keep saying the latest phrase so you sound good."

"I hope you're exaggerating."

"'Fraid not."

"I suspect this is the real reason why men are the masters of the universe."

"Are we?"

"According to Figgy, you are. And now I know why. You're all afraid of looking stupid."

"Yep."

"How depressing."

"So - can I come over and cheer you up?"

"When?"

"I'm not doing anything this weekend. I thought I could book a B&B -"

"I've got room at my house."

"You've got a spare room?"

"No, not exactly. I've got a double bed, though."

"Won't Nancy mind?"

"We'll talk about it."

So here I was, rushing it again, in spite of all my resolutions to the contrary, unfortunately I just couldn't wait to get the man's trousers off. If only I had Carla to talk to, she would give me good advice. I really missed Carla. I still couldn't believe she had just done a runner with my money, I was sure she wasn't the type. Whatever the type was.

The problem was resolved without my having to do anything, because Nancy went to spend the night with a friend. This time I made sure I rang the mother of the friend, to check that Nancy was doing just that.

"Hello, is this Susan? I'm Holly, Nancy's mother."

"Hello, Nancy's here, they're tucked up on the sofa watching Fight Club," said a maternal voice.

"Splendid, thank you, I hope she's no trouble, maybe we'll meet at Parent's Evening one day. Or evening. Or something. Thank you, goodbye," I babbled.

"This is the perfect opportunity to visit that pub, the one Figgy says the sleazebag takes his little ladies to," I said to Steve. He appeared to be slightly less than thrilled by this romantic prospect.

"Undercover super sleuths," I said, "look, we can't let Figgy get all the glory. He's far too big for his boots as it is. In fact he's too big for most of his clothes."

"Alright, then, as long as we can have a nice meal as well. I don't want to spend all evening in a smoky hell hole, even with you."

"We used to spend a lot of our evenings in smoky hell holes once," I murmured nostalgically, "do you remember those bonfires we used to make and our inefficient attempts at baked potatoes?

The builders must have been furious when they came back in the morning and found our efforts in the middle of the half-built lounge."

"Yes but we were young and foolish, and we couldn't afford anything nicer. Now we can."

"Shall we eat first and go to the hell hole afterwards?"

We did. Over dinner I found out a lot more about Steve, and, finally, why he wasn't married. It was a tragic tale. He had been married, once, when he was much younger, and his wife had run away with his best friend. Three years later, she had come back, with a young son (the son of the best friend) in tow, begging him to take her back, and Steve had done his best to make the marriage work again. But, just as they were rebuilding some trust and starting to have fun, she had discovered she had breast cancer. The next five years had been a long battle against the disease, which had gone into remission, but tragically returned. After her death, Steve's former best friend had come to reclaim his son. Steve had put up a fight, and there was what sounded like an acrimonious fight, before the best friend had won the ensuing court battle. Then Steve had no-one left.

"That's so sad," I said unnecessarily.

"Yes."

"Much worse than my story about how my marriage ended."

"Much worse."

"In fact, it makes mine look almost amusing in comparison."

"Steady on."

"Do you ever see your stepson?"

"Nope. Not because I don't want to, mind."

"I'm so sorry."

"Yeah, well. I'm sorry too."

There was a thoughtful silence.

"I lost a child too," I suddenly blurted out.

"Oh no. Holly."

"I don't usually mention it."

"What happened?"

"Well."

Suddenly I couldn't talk about it. I wished I hadn't mentioned it, I was only doing attempting one-upmanship in the tragedy department. How horrible was I?

"Can I tell you another time?"

"Of course." He took my hand and looked at me with that sudden intensity again.

"I don't know about you, but the hell hole is calling me."

The hell hole turned out to be a slightly seedy but not nasty pub. If you were feeling generous you would describe it as quirky. I could see why Graeme used it for his assignations, because it had lots of low beams, dark corners and high backed benches, so I had to pretend to wander around looking for the Ladies' in order to establish that he wasn't there.

"Let's have one drink and go," I suggested.

Steve pronounced himself satisfied with the house ale and I ordered a mineral water, so as to keep my mind clear.

We settled at the bar, where we had a good view of the door.

"It's odd, this thing about knowing you and not knowing you."

"And trusting you and not trusting you," I said.

"As if I dreamed you," he went on.

"Don't get soppy," I warned, "or I'll start to suspect you're not really a Yorkshireman. What football team do you support?"

"Leeds, of course."

"Thank God for that."

"I didn't remember that you liked football?"

"Well, you wouldn't. But I do. And I support Leeds too."

"I can keep my matching Leeds United duvet cover and curtains then? Gotcha," he added as he saw my face.

There weren't many other people in the pub, no music, and it had gone very quiet just where we were when suddenly the door opened and Graeme came in with a very young looking girl. I hid my face behind Steve but hissed instructions to him.

"See where they sit! What do you think? How old is that girl?"

"About twelve, I should say."

"No, seriously! What if she's just a very young looking teacher?"

"Seriously, she's not more than sixteen. The creep. How old is he?"

"I'm not sure. Thirty something, I think."

"Bastard."

I had my camera phone, but Steve's was better (typical) and could make a short video. With sound. We had a plan.

"Hello, it's Mr Birch, isn't it?"

He looked up. Behind his thick glasses his eyes were panicky, like a sheep who sees a dog.

"Have we met?"

"You taught my daughter last year? I met you at parent's evening?"

What was it with these Australian sentence endings?

"Oh, yes, of course, Mrs, er -"

"Ms Field."

"Oh yes."

He couldn't think who I was. Good. The girl at his side was looking nervous too, clutching her alcopop as if it was an ice lolly. She was probably fifteen or sixteen but was the shy, quiet, vulnerable type who looked younger.

"Graeme -" she began.

"Just wait," he said, holding up his hand.

"Still waiting for her results, of course," I went on, as if chatting, "but I'm sure she'll do fine. She spoke very highly of you."

"Oh, good, good, that's excellent," he said.

A rat in a trap.

"Is this one of your pupils?" I enquired, indicating his companion. "I was told you go out of your way to make young people feel confident about their studies."

"No, no, this is my, um, um, niece," he stuttered.

"It was nice to meet you," I said, and went innocently back to the bar.

"He hasn't the faintest idea who I am," I said triumphantly. "Did you get the pictures?"

"Got the girl in close up with the label on her bottle clearly visible."

"Fantastic!"

We supped up and sped home. It was much better this time. We had all night to get to know each other really well. He kissed me in places I was fairly sure I had never been kissed before. I forgot who he was, where I was and what my name was. It had never been like that before.

However, one good thing was, I had managed not to fall in love. So when Steve failed to call me the next day or the next or the one after that or indeed, the one after that, I was not distraught. I was pissed off, but I was not distraught. It was par for the course. When, oh when would I learn?

My main concern was for the video of Mr Sneak Features. I would have to ring Steve to get hold of it. But he hadn't rung me. So I couldn't ring him. Damn, damn. After a couple of days of this fretting I decided it was too ridiculously adolescent for words, and that I should just ring him and demand my evidence and, oh, by the way, tell him I never wanted to see him again, either.

But it was another couple of days after that before I got the courage to do it. And even then I had to drink two glasses of wine, oh alright then two thirds of a bottle.

"Hello? It's the Aston Martin helpline. Thing. Again. Ringing you, how is that for service?"

"I never did get that part."

"Do you actually own an Aston Martin? I'm beginning to doubt it."

"I own parts of one. Almost a whole one. In time I hope to get into some sort of drivable condition. It's a long term plan. I'm glad you rang, by the way, I was going to ring you but I was hesitating because I thought you might be a bit cross with me."

"And why would I be cross? At all? Obviously I'm not cross. I'm fine."

"Because I hadn't rung you."

"Oh. I see. And. So."

"You see, I've been ill all this week, and I couldn't even get out of bed for three days. I think it was flu."

"Very convincing."

"No, really, it's true. And because I live on my own I couldn't get a message to you. I tried to text but the phone kept falling out of my hand. And then I thought you might think I wasn't ringing because you'd slept with me."

"At least you know the etiquette. But I absolutely don't believe you. It's just too bloody convenient."

"It wasn't convenient for me."

"Well how come I'm not ill then?"

"Maybe you're going down with it. Incubation period must be just about up."

I laughed shortly. "I doubt I have much to fear from your mythical disease. Anyway, all I want is that video. Can you email it to me?"

"Of course. So - are you saying you don't want to see me again?"

"Yes, I am. Goodbye."

There. I was firm and decisive, I hadn't fallen in love and I hadn't got hurt. I knew I could do it. Two days later I was in bed with the most appalling flu. I couldn't eat, speak or move for three days. A big bunch of flowers arrived. Carnation, lily, lily, rose. I had a temperature of 104. Nothing made much sense.

"There's a card," Nancy said, bringing them to my bedside.

I made a croaking noise.

"Shall I read it?"

"Ribbit."

"That reminds me of a joke about a chicken who goes into a library. And says 'book book book'. Then the chicken goes to see this frog -" All I could do was attempt to glare at her, which hurt my eyes and made me cough.

"Card says, 'hope you didn't catch anything nasty from kissing me. I seem to be suffering from love sickness.' Then a lot of kisses -" she counted them - "Eleven. That's quite sweet I suppose. I'll put them in a vase for you. Do you want some soup?"

I shook my head feebly and went back to sleep, only to have horrible feverish dreams about chickens, frogs and sick roses and phones ringing frantically. I woke up and the phone was ringing frantically. I heard Nancy go to answer it.

"What." It was not so much a question as a statement. Thus she had answered the phone since she was three. "Oh, no, you can't, she's not available at the moment, bye." I went back to sleep. It was all I could do.

Chapter 17

Monkey Feather

When I finally returned to the sunlit lands from the pit of death in which I had found myself, I was a little confused about what was going on. I stumbled round the house in convalescent mode wearing my old grey dressing gown and smelling ill. I ate miso soup and listened to Radiohead and the late quartets of Beethoven, because that was the frame of mind I was in. For a day I pondered my life's direction. The big questions. The questions now uppermost in my mind were:

Where was Nancy going to live? And what school was she going to?

Did I have a job? No-one had informed Figgy of my illness so possibly he had replaced me with a new dynamic assistant.

Where was I going to buy a house?

Did I want to see Steve again? No, of course I didn't, silly question, him with his supposed tragic life and phony illness. So the illness may have been true, but did that make any difference?

And where was bloody Carla when I needed her to run all these things past her?

First things first.

"Nance? What school do you want to go to?"

She looked at me as if I was mad.

"My school, of course. School."

"So, do you want to live with me, or your dad?"

"Mostly with you. Well, if dad's going to have girlfriends. Especially ones like Mimi."

"What's so wrong with Mimi. She can't be all that bad? I think it's quite brave of her to ask you to wash up."

"She laughs at all his jokes. Even the ones that aren't funny. And anyway, she's called Mimi."

"Oh, I see. Fine, that's settled. You can live with me, and go to your school. But no more horrible old boyfriends, OK?"

"Like you can talk."

I phoned Figgy.

"Hello, Mr Lamb?"

"Don't you dare call me that. And where the hell have you been?"

I explained.

"So get your arse down here this morning, I'm up to my wobbly bits in bits of paper and I haven't had a decent lunch for a bloody week."

"Have I still got a job, then?"

"If you don't get here soon, none of us will have a job. I'm simply not built for solo flight."

While at work I pondered my other questions. But the main one was: Why is my life so complicated?

After a lunch of exceptionally refreshing quality and length, Figgy returned in the afternoon more talkative than usual.

"Met a chap, knows your Eyetie lady."

"Don't say that, Figgy, or I'll leave."

"Sorry, sorry, political correctness of course, Italian lady then."

"Woman. Italian woman. I met a man who knows the Italian woman of whom we spoke."

"Did you?"

"No, I'm just saying how you should have said that instead of 'your Italian lady.'"

"Isn't lady politer than woman?"

"No."

"I always thought it was," said Figgy, looking puzzled.

"That's because you went to a public school in the fifties."

"So it was politer then?"

"Probably."

"But not now?"

"No. Not since the seventies. Possibly different rules apply in Yorkshire."

Figgy's brain was not really in a fit state for this kind of debate. He frowned, and sat down heavily in his swivelling leatherette chair. I sighed.

"It's like this," I said, "I'll try to explain. What do women get called in porn mags?"

Figgy brightened. He knew the answer to this one.

"Girls."

"Exactly. And if they're getting on a bit, or a bit ugly?"

Figgy thought.

"Dogs?" he suggested.

"Or?"

"Ladies."

"Precisely. What are they never called?"

"I give up."

"Women. They're never called women. So we call ourselves that. It's like nigger, or paki."

"Now you've completely lost me."

I sighed again. There was a short pause and then Figgy reverted to the previous point.

"Anyway, chap says she went abroad in a hurry, but he thinks she left an address."

"Where?"

"Chap, friend of Mungo's, didn't know where she'd gone."

"No, I mean, where did she leave the address?"

"No idea, but I told the chap to find out and I'd sort him out some rubber wear for the missus."

"Does she know?"

"Surprise," said Figgy, grinning evilly.

This conversation had taken so much out of him that he slept for the rest of the afternoon, not even waking up for the special consignment from Amsterdam which he had been so eager to see.

The day of Nancy's results arrived and I still hadn't done anything about Steve. The email with the video had arrived and I had failed to acknowledge it. I still wasn't buying the dead wife and the sudden illness stuff, it was all far too convenient. And therefore suspicious in itself. Oooh it was annoying. I had thought he was so fabulous. It was Roger all over again.

I now had the video on my laptop and, as this was the first day that school had been open since the debacle in France, I was keen to take it to show Miss Bligh. However, it would have been impossible to do this without arousing Nancy's suspicions so I decided to take a different tack.

We drove up to Nancy's school, a forbidding soot-blackened building lurking behind an avenue of depressed poplars which I normally avoided. It gave me the creeps, because it was so like my own old school. Nancy loved it. She was in a surprisingly good mood. I had expected to be given a hard time today, because Nancy was always tricky when she was stressed. She jumped out of the car and disappeared into a sea of girls waving pieces of paper as soon as I slowed on the approach. I parked and sauntered over to the main hall, trying to look as if I wasn't all that bothered what her results were. Results, who cares? Secretly, I was sweating with fear.

Suddenly I noticed a familiar face - where had I seen that girl before - she wasn't one of Nancy's friends? Then I realised - it was the girl from the pub with Graeme. Frantically I looked around for my daughter. Where was she when I needed her? Oh, there she was.

"You needn't panic, mum," she said, seeing my face, "I got ten A stars and a B."

"Hooray, hooray," I shouted, leaping about, and then stopped. "What was the B in?"

She looked at me to check that I was joking.

"Technology."

"Well thank God you don't want to be a technologist, that's all I can say."

All around us lovely young women were leaping in the air in celebration or huddled in corners, weeping. In either state they looked sensationally lovely. A photographer form the local paper was seeking out the most pneumatic in order to take shots of them on their mobiles, relaying the good news. I felt a bit sad and old. I looked around for the girl from the pub. There she was, by the stage, with a woman who was presumably her mother.

"Nancy," I hissed, grabbing her arm, "who's that girl, over there in the pink, with the woman in green?"

Nancy looked.

"Oh, her. That's Amber Fawcett. She's OK. I don't really know her, she does drama and all that. Was going to be some big part in the school play, I think. Her dad died though, it's a bit sad. So I don't think she's doing it now."

So. Another fatherless young woman. How convenient for Mr Birch. I expect he has devised all sorts of special comforting techniques, the bastard.

I sought out Miss Bligh. She wasn't difficult to spot. Her outfit today surpassed even her usual standards of sartorial outrageousness, consisting as it did of a kind of Miss Marpleon-acid look, tweed with neon accessories.

"Oh, hasn't Nancy done well, I'm so pleased for her, you see you needn't have worried."

As she spoke her earrings flashed on and off. One said PUNK and the other said ROCK.

"Actually, Miss Bligh, I need to talk to you about something quite worrying concerning Nancy. I would like to make an appointment to come and see you, please."

"Of course," Miss Bligh said, getting a bit flustered and dropping her pink neon pen, "when would be a good time?"

"Lunchtime, any day."

"Wednesday?"

"Fine."

I dragged Nancy away from the photographer who was trying to pose her by the gym horse, and forced her grimly into the car.

I went to work and bragged about my daughter all day. Piece by piece, the patchwork of my life started to look as if it was going to form a pattern. I was moving forwards, moving on, learning not to trust anyone. I was invincible. But was that absolutely true? Was I not, for example, trusting Figgy rather too much?

He had been a bit miffed, he told me, that I had taken Steve to the pub to do the super sleuthing instead of him, and now insisted that he was allowed to join in the Carla hunt. Having heard the full story, he, like Basil before him, was concerned that I had been conned.

"She saw you coming. Innocent, vulnerable. There are lots of predatory women out there, believe me, I meet 'em all the time." He sighed. "Chap in my position has to be careful. Just be grateful she isn't a man. Then you might be in real trouble. You'd think five thou was a drop in the ocean, if some unprincipled rogue got his hands on you." "I honestly don't think -"

"Far too trusting," he said, shaking his head and echoing my thoughts.

"Well, I trust you. Is that stupid of me?"

"Ah, well, that's something else. You can trust me in most departments," Figgy's voice heaved with emotion, "except where the heart is concerned. Like most chaps, I am susceptible to the charms of the ladies."

"Women."

"Sorry, yes, women." He looked abashed, then brightened as a thought struck him.

"When can you come and meet my chap with the address, Holly? I want to know what happens next! Let's make a date!"

Uh oh, now I had a date with Figgy.

Now, in rapid succession, I dealt with my demons. First up, Miss Bligh. I parked at the school, heaving on my handbrake with such determination that I was going to have trouble getting away. I stumped up the driveway, poplars to right and left, bloody school. I went in. It smelled of sweaty trainers, cabbage and polish, like all schools. I felt sick.

"Come in," Miss Bligh tweeted. "How lovely to see you. Didn't Nancy do well in her exams? I'm so looking forward to seeing her in the sixth next term."

"Yes, yes," I said impatiently.

"And how are you doing with sorting out your marriage?"

Now she was on dangerous territory.

"I told you, I have got divorced."

"Oh, no, what a shame. I was so sure that it was only a hiccup."

"Hiccup?"

"Yes," Miss Bligh twittered on, seemingly oblivious to my rage. "I always think it's so much better for children to have two parents."

"She has got two parents."

"Two parents living together, I mean."

"Even if they're the same sex?"

"Don't be foolish, my dear, in that case they couldn't be the parents."

I sighed. My one-woman mission to introduce political correctness to Yorkshire was a Sisyphean labour.

I heaved my laptop onto her desk. What was Miss Bligh wearing? Well. Today she was wearing a sort of Nazi uniform accessorized with dangly diamante earrings and over-the180 knee lace-up boots. I was not intimidated.

"I want you to watch this video, made in a local public house. I want you to look closely."

"I fail to see the -"

"This film shows one of your teachers, Mr Birch, giving alcohol to an under-age pupil in a pub," I said sternly. "A minor," I added. I felt like a BBC undercover reporter. Only with an audience of one.

"I don't really see why this is any of your business," Miss Bligh said, coldly. This made me very angry. I stood up in my agitation, and paced the horrible green school carpet. I did not want to hit Miss Bligh. Particularly as she was even older than I was.

"Well first of all because I have a daughter at this school, and I hope I have the welfare of all the pupils at heart," I said, coldly but nobly, "but also and more importantly because the little shit has been knobbing my daughter."

Miss Bligh looked a bit shocked, more by my language than my revelation I suspected, and rang her secretary to get a cup of tea sent in.

"Please calm down, Mrs -"

"Ms." I corrected her. "Ms Field. Please try to get my name right in future."

"Do you have any proof?"

"She told me. In front of witnesses as it happens. But she won't make an official complaint. However, here you can see evidence that he's preying on other young girls."

"Amber is sixteen."

"Oh, well, that's alright then," I said sarcastically.

Miss Bligh's manner suddenly changed with startling speed. Her face crumpled and she burst into tears and threw her head into her hands in a most unnecessarily theatrical manner.

"Think what a scandal this will be for the school if it gets out! I beg you, on my knees Muzz Field, don't do this to my beloved school! This school is my life!"

At this point the tea was brought in and Miss Bligh suddenly snapped out of it, wiping her eyes and smiling bravely.

"Thank you, Dorothy," she said graciously, as the secretary left the room backwards, her body slightly inclined in a half bow, whether to keep an eye on me or as an homage to Miss Bligh, I couldn't say.

"Look, Miss Bligh," I said, "I care about the reputation of the school as well, because in case you'd forgotten you've just accepted my daughter into the sixth form. I want her to be very happy there. I haven't gone to the police, because I wanted to talk to you first. Now stop all this emotional blackmail stuff and let's work out how to get rid of the disgusting little man."

Miss Bligh calmed down, and, picking up a lorgnette which was lying on her desk, she looked at me through it. Was there no end to her eccentricities?

"Righty-ho, Muzz Field," she said. "Let's talk. Let's cut to the mustard."

"Let me show you the video, first."

It was a good video. The close up of the alcopop clutched in a tiny hand with bitten fingernails was particularly effective. The child looked sweet and vulnerable and a lot younger than sixteen. Graeme looked particularly old and creepy. After we had watched it, Miss Bligh wiped away a tear, and turned to me. A new steeliness now glittered in her eye.

"You're right. I don't want to let this go on," she said. "I confess this is not the first time I have had suspicions about Graeme, but I have never had evidence before. Now we can act."

Then Figgy and I went to meet Mungo and Mungo's chap at the golf club, as I might have guessed. The golf club itself was a deeply depressing sixties bungalow style building with comfy floral chairs and sofas and a bamboo-effect bar. It was surrounded by a deeply depressing golf course with fat men in buggies driving self-importantly across it. These were visible through the huge French windows which were not improved by immense and hideous curtains the height of juggernauts and the colour of sick. I was feeling a little uncharitable.

All the other ladies there, and they were ladies, even I had to admit, wore pleated skirts and clip on pearl earrings. I was wearing jeans and a rather nice pink top. It was completely wrong. There weren't many ladies, though, most of the clientele were red faced portly chaps like Figgy, Mungo and Mungo's chap, who turned out to be my old red-faced friend Ian from the village. Though of course I was always really more friends with Maggie, than Ian. He was rather embarrassed to see me. Actually tremendously embarrassed.

"Holly - I had no idea it was you - ! You won't say anything to Maggie?"

"There's not much danger of that, she never returns my calls these days. I'm not much use to her any more, I guess," I said a little bitterly, because it was true that I had really thought that Maggie was my friend, and that I was more to her than coffee morning fodder.

We sat around a glass topped coffee table on the deep sofas (it was quite an effort to lean forward to pick up one's glass) and I met Mungo, who seemed quite a lot like Figgy. They had been to the same prep school, which explained a lot. Ian was still shuffling a bit nervously, as the time approached when he would have to tell me what he knew about Carla.

"So," I began, when all the formalities appeared to be over and I had been settled with a glass of white wine instead of the pint of Timothy Taylor I had requested.

"Ladies don't drink that kind of thing in here," Mungo explained. "In fact, the bar staff won't serve a lady a pint of anything, and even a half pint is frowned upon. Unless it's in a special ladies' half pint glass, and it's shandy or something."

However there were apparently no such restrictions on spirits so most of the ladies, sensibly, were on treble gins.

I looked meaningfully at Figgy but he was frowning thoughtfully into his whisky glass and took not a scrap of notice. There was a short silence while we all took sips of our drinks. Then I shuffled my bottom back into the sofa.

"So," I began again, "Ian, what do you know about Carla?"

Ian's face, always an unhealthy sweet-pea pink, was now verging on peony.

"Met her at your do," he began, as if it all my fault.

"And?"

"Sort of kept in touch."

"I see. But -"

"We were quite close, for a while. I lent her a few quid, so naturally I wanted to keep an eye on her."

"So why hasn't she kept in touch with me?"

"Well, she didn't want to talk to you."

"Why the hell not?" I said rather loudly.

Several golf club members looked round in disgust at this profanity.

"Language, lovey," Figgy said. "But, we have to be honest, we all know the Eyeties are slippery customers, don't we? Famous for it."

This sort of language on the other hand was perfectly acceptable and the ladies sipped their gin and tonics unperturbed.

"Thing is," Ian said, "things are dragging on a bit, apparently, and she didn't want to talk to you until she had your money. Our money. She's embarrassed. She's not talking to me, either, at the moment. Can't get a reply at all."

"Oh, I expect Figgy's right," I exclaimed, "she saw us coming and I'll never get it back." "I'm sure she means to," Ian said, "but look - here - anyway, here's her address in Tanzania if you want to contact her. I've given up trying to contact her. Anyway, it was only a grand."

"I'm glad you can be so relaxed about it!"

"Well, you try contacting her."

"What if she's dead?"

"Waste of time, old girl," Figgy said, "trust me, I have an instinct about women and money. She's not dead, just done a bunk."

"You've not met her."

"Yes, but I'm over familiar with the type," he said, and all the men laughed ruefully, including some at the next table. How rude, I thought, but this seemed to be a place where what I thought was rude was polite, and vice versa, so I kept quiet.

"Well, you know what," I said, getting out of the depths of the sofa with some difficulty, rising indignantly to my feet and preparing to wipe the dust of the golf club from my inappropriately shod feet, "I think you're all wrong. I'd put money on it, but I'd feel guilty about taking it off you."

Ignoring their pitying expressions, I got the hell out of there. Nancy, meanwhile, knew nothing about my subterfuge with Miss Bligh and I began to feel guilty about hiding it from her, but what could I do? I was more and more anxious for someone to talk to about it all, so eventually, in desperation, I rang Steve.

"Hello?" It was that voice again. Got me every time, like a kick in the stomach.

"Hello."

"Not the Aston Martin helpline today?"

"Couldn't help anyone today. I need help today."

"So you rang me?"

"Because you already know all about Nancy and the pervert teacher."

"Which is the only reason you rang me? I've left countless messages on your phone -"

"Yes, I know. I know. I've deleted them all. I've been here before. With men. The thing is, I don't really believe you. You're too good to be true, and one of my first rules is, if a man seems too perfect then he probably isn't."

"I promise you, Holly," he said, and his voice went very low indeed, and sort of reliable, or was it? "I am very far from perfect. Do you want me to list my faults?"

"Er -"

"Or would you rather find them all out for yourself, one by one? Gradually?"

"Let's talk about something else," I said hastily.

"Can I come over and talk to you, face to face? Please?"

I wanted to say no, really I did.

Chapter 18

Mr Brown is at the window

So I was very startled indeed when the next moment there was a loud and testosterone fuelled banging on my front door. Surely it couldn't be Steve yet? Unless he had been outside all along...? And then the light momentarily dimmed as a shadow loomed at the window. Who was peering into my house in this presumptuous manner?

I should have known.

"What do you want?" I enquired ungraciously.

"Can I come in?" he snapped.

It was the first time I had seen him for months. He had put on weight.

"Mimi's looking after you," I remarked.

"There's no need to be unpleasant," he said.

"Was I?"

"Let's not start anything, shall we?"

"I suppose you've come about Nancy? There's no need, I've sorted it out. She doesn't know, but it's over."

"Oh, well, of course, " be began hastily and unconvincingly, "I would have done something... only you were on the spot, as it were -"

"Yes," I said. "On the spot."

I turned my back and walked toward the kitchen, and he followed me.

"I need to talk to you about - a lot of things," he said, to my ears ominously.

"What kind of things?"

"Nancy says you have a boyfriend."

"So?"

"Where is he? I want a word. Look. I'm not paying maintenance for some sponging arsehole to put his feet up on my sofa and watch Skysports all day."

"What are you talking about? I don't even have Sky!"

"That won't stop him. I know the type. Nancy's given me enough information for me to get the whole bloody picture. She doesn't understand, of course, but I can read between the lines."

He was getting himself all worked up now and turning a funny colour.

"I do wish you'd just spit it out. Just come to the point. What's bothering you?"

"All right. I want you to know that I am going to see my solicitor about this."

All the time he was peering around him as if he expected Steve to be hiding in one of the kitchen cupboards. I put the kettle on, hoping that Steve would not rush over. I was mentally working out the earliest he could get here, given the traffic and that he might have had some little jobs to do before he set off, so I wasn't really listening.

" - I'm sorry, I didn't catch that."

He was going through the old-fashioned sweet pea shades with remarkable speed.

" - bad influence on my daughter, sponging off my money and no doubt tarnishing my name -"

I laughed shortly. "Tarnishing your name? Are you completely mad? He doesn't even know you. And don't you think you did a good enough job all by yourself?"

"I don't know what you've been telling people -"

"The truth."

"Oh - you've told them how you stitched me up, have you?"

"I - what - ?"

I was speechless. The kettle boiled.

"So called divorce. I call it a miscarriage of justice. I earned all that bloody money, every damn penny of it, and don't you forget it. And if you think some jumped up little northern scally is getting his hands on it, you'll find you've got a fight on." He was puffing a bit, and I feared for his health. I made him a cup of tea, and sat down at the table.

"Look," I said, trying to sound reasonable, "I can see you're upset. But Steve doesn't live here, and doesn't have any plans to move in. And actually, it's none of your business. So drink your tea and then go home, there's a good chap. Mimi will be wondering what's happened to you."

He started to splutter unintelligibly at this, and I had to wipe some spots of spit off my kitchen table. As I put the cloth back in the sink, I felt that I was not handling things very well. How on earth was I going to get rid of him?

"I have to go to the loo," I said, and locking the door behind me I began frantically texting Steve to tell him to hold off for a bit. This took me so long that the banging on the door started again, this time on the loo door about three inches from my ear. I was so startled that I leapt into the air and my phone fell down the loo. Oh God. I didn't think the text had sent. I began to fish round the bend to get the damn thing out.

"What are you doing in there? Is everything ok? Look, come out will you? I need you to sign something."

I had retrieved the phone so I left it on the towel rail to dry. It looked a bit dead. Back in the kitchen, he had spread out a piece of paper and thoughtfully provided a biro.

"What's this?"

"I want you to agree that, if your fancy man moves in, you'll forego your maintenance payments."

"Forego? Herewith? From henceforth?"

"Just shut the fuck up and sign it."

"Hmmm."

I read his piece of paper.

"Ok, why the hell not, if it'll keep you happy. He's not moving in, anyway, so it doesn't make any difference."

"I'll be watching you."

"As Sting so apparently romantically sang."

I signed, and hoped he would go now. No such luck. Now he tucked the contract into his pocket and started wandering round the house, picking up random knick-knacks.

"This is mine. I bought it. In Mont St Michel. I remember buying it. It's definitely mine."

"Well, why don't you take it. Look - here's a carrier bag. Do you want anything else?"

"I might."

He just carried on prowling like a particularly worked-up caged tiger.

"When's Nancy home?"

"She's staying with a friend tonight."

"How convenient."

"I wish you'd stop going on like this. I'm not even -" I paused.

"What? You're not even what?"

"Not even sure I want to go out with Steve," I confessed.

"That's not what I hear," he sneered. "I hear you're all over him like a particularly unpleasant rash."

There was another silence, while we both sipped our tea. It had gone cold. The silence became heavy with something.

"Mimi's pregnant," he said suddenly.

"Nancy will be thrilled," I said.

"I wish -" he began, but did not go on. "Holly," he said. He looked at me with an expression which reminded me of a troll I had owned when I was twelve. It had had orange hair. I decided not to encourage him to go on.

"Mimi will be needing you," I said.

"Yes."

Horror! I heard a mighty roaring sound which seemed to mean that the Aston Martin might have been pressed into service. I looked nervously out of the window, and there it was. Oh, hell.

"Aha!" he said with a bellow of rage and rushed outside. Steve was just getting out of the car.

"Now, listen, you wanker -"

But Steve was not in the mood for listening. He just held him at arm's length, which was conveniently distant enough to prevent injury.

"Holly," Steve said, his voice slightly raised over the muffled cries, "I thought we might go out to eat. Did you want any little jobs doing while you get changed?"

"Why, thank you, Steve," I said. "I'll leave it with you."

A little later, I was finally in the Aston Martin, heading for a lovely meal with a lovely man. I was basking in happiness.

"What was all that about?"

"oh, he wanted me to sign something."

"What?"

"oh, nothing."

"Come on, you can tell me."

The car was gliding (effortlessly!) through surreally beautiful landscapes as we conversed. I was disinclined to talk about disagreeable things, when everything else was so delightful.

"Do we have to?"

There was a short pause, and for a moment I thought I had motored breezily on and left the unpleasant topic behind.

"Was it money?"

I took a deep breath. "Yes."

"And he said -?"

"He said I had to sign a thing to say I won't expect any maintenance if I cohabit."

"And did you?"
"Yep."
"Why?"
"Because - well - it's none of your business."
"It might be."

There was another pause, which was saved from being a silence by Blur, who were in the background. It seemed appropriate.

"As a matter of fact," he began.
"What?"
"I was thinking," he went on infuriatingly slowly.
"What?"
(Pause)
"What were you thinking, for God's sake?"
"That I would like to live with you."
"Oh." Thank God, he'd said it. Oh the relief.
"But, now -"
"What? What do you mean, now?"
"Now that you've signed this thing..."

Oh God! That was it! It was all ruined! Just what he would have wanted, of course, the bastard. Now everything was over.

"Yes, I suppose it complicates things."
"Yes. Now we're going to have to get married."
"What?"
"Will you stop saying what?"
"I think I misheard you."
"WILL YOU MARRY ME?" he bellowed.
"YES!" I bellowed back.

Chapter 19

A Map of Africa

Picture me, now, in shorts in the bush. Not the bush I fell into outside that pub, but the African bush. In Africa. I am trekking along with a group of people, who include Nancy and Steve, among others. How has this come about? Well, it's like this. Gosh, where do I start?

Here I am, and not five yards away are three adult warthogs, bristling with indignation. And I thought Figgy was prickly. Figgy has nothing on a warthog. The whole group of us pauses, and contemplates the warthogs. We stand in a bunch, looking. The warthogs look at us. They are unimpressed, and rather hostile than otherwise. Steve, rather carelessly I feel, takes photos. I am sure that the warthogs do not like having their photos taken. I want to tell you how I got here, but it's impossible to leave the here and now, just now, because at any moment some wild and beautiful animal might take it into it's head to leap on us and devour/trample/gore or otherwise mutilate one or all of our party. I need to concentrate.

Our guide, who has tribal markings on his face ("how cool is that?" said Nancy) and a rifle casually slung over his shoulder (and what use would that be if a herd of elephants were to decide to charge? Ha? said Holly) decides to move off at this point. We follow, some of us still (insensitively, how could they?) taking photos. Phew. We are in the shade of an acacia, glugging from our water bottles, apart from Steve that is, as he has a water pouch thing in his rucksack from which he can sip any time via a giant straw arrangement. He is such a show-off. The only immediate threat to our well-being is from giant ants who live in the thorns. Nancy is entranced by the ants. I can think clearly, for a few moments.

Figgy was quite instrumental in all this, but Figgy is not with us. Sadly, just before we left England Figgy was whisked into hospital for a heart bypass operation. He wouldn't hear of us postponing our honeymoon, so we didn't. Latest news is that he is making a full recovery, but has been told to lay off the booze. Poor Figgy.

Did I say honeymoon? Well, I meant to say. We got married in a bit of a rush, and came out here to meet Carla. Oh, now I'm really confusing things. I can see I need to go back a bit, though not much. It took about three days before it was all arranged. Even Nancy could see that it was right, and she doesn't normally like sharing me with anyone.

"You've gone all shiny, mum," she said, "It's lovely. I like you like this. Just don't fall out with him. And don't bully him. He's so nice, I think you could get away with anything. Be nice to him."

She was the only bridesmaid, in a brown silk dress (like mine) and we got married quietly, just a few family members and friends. No religion was involved at any stage. My mother couldn't make it, as she was in Zanzibar. Jane's boys all came to the wedding and behaved impeccably, to everyone's astonishment. Especially Jane's. My dad turned up, saying he couldn't stop as he was on his way to Scotland for an old boys' reunion. However, he got on so well with Figgy that he stayed drinking with him for the whole day and was possibly partly responsible for Figgy's subsequent collapse during the frenzied dancing to Dancing Queen, in which he had overconfidently joined. But as dad was long gone up the misty glens I couldn't berate him for it. And in any case it had been nice to see him, for the first time in three years. And Figgy's number was probably up anyway.

Luckily it was only a minor heart attack ("shot across the bows") and the doctor assured us, as we clustered anxiously in Accident and Emergency in our wedding clothes, that he would be fine as long as he made some drastic lifestyle changes. Oh dear. But, as I already said, Figgy insisted that we should come away on honeymoon, so here we are. On safari at the moment, but meeting Carla and mum tomorrow. I'm just grateful Steve didn't meet my mother before we got married, or he might have changed his mind.

Nancy still doesn't know about Mr Birch. She'll find out next term, I suppose. He has been fired, following a private hearing, and Miss Bligh is going to word his references in such a way that he'll never work with children again. We hope. I'm keeping a copy of the video, just in case. But I couldn't go to the police after Miss Bligh had gone down on her bended arthritic knees and begged me to save the reputation of the school. Could I? I may have nightmares about this, in the future.

Will Nancy ever forgive me? I think she will. She has a new boyfriend, called Ben. He is her age! He plays the bassoon in the school orchestra, and is therefore almost de facto suitable. I didn't even need to meet him. But I have met him. I liked him very much. He has long hair and I suspect his roll-ups of being filled with tobacco plus. Oh dear. Like I would know what suitable is. But his father is a solicitor, and his mother is a GP. What a lovely boy.

We are advancing through the bush once more. Ahead of us, through the trees, there is a lot of movement all of a sudden. The guide motions us to keep still. We freeze.

"Elephants, coming up from the river. See? The matriarch. She has a baby."

"Aaaah," some of us say. "How cute." I'm not one of them. I know how she feels.

"She is very dangerous. The baby is very small. The mother will defend her calf to the death. If she puts her ears out, she is preparing to charge. We must be cautious." As he spoke the lead elephant opened her ears out like Dumbo about to take off and fly away.

"Scatter," hissed the guide. "Small groups, under the trees." I grabbed Nancy's hand and we stood under a nearby tree. Don't ask me what kind of tree, I was gibbering with fear. Where was Steve when I needed him? Oh, there he was, just behind me. We were a small group of three. The guide was over there, with his trusty rifle, not that it would be much use against a charging herd of ELEPHANTS. I am psychic. I knew this would happen. We cling together, well, that is, I grab Nancy and Steve in a group hug. They seem strangely calm. The elephants move off, flapping their ears contemptuously. Why is all the wildlife so arrogant? Maybe it is for show, like youths in hoodies. I gradually relax. My heart rate slows down. I drink some water.

"Weren't you scared?"

"Not at all."

"Bah."

"It's part of the show, isn't it? Like the rides at Disneyland giving the illusion of danger."

"Ha." The guide, gun and tribal markings and all (he still made me a bit nervous) came over to join us under our tree.

"We will have a break now."

"Oh good."

"That was a good view of elephants."

"Ha. Gosh, you're very cam about all this, aren't you?"

"It's my job," he said modestly.

"Yes but, don't you ever get scared - frightened?"

"No," he said.

I was silenced by his certainty.

"So, what part of England are you from? London?" he enquired.

"No, north -" I gestured upwards, as if that helped, " in the north of England. You wouldn't know it."

"Where is that, then? Manchester?"

"No, the other side, near a place called Leeds. In Yorkshire."

"Ah, Leeds United," he said, a great white joyous smile breaking out and enlightenment spreading over his face, "they should never have got rid of David O'Leary. It has been all downhill since then."

"Too true," said Steve, behind me.

We are now in a restaurant in Dar es Salaam, with impala, among other lovely wild creatures, on the menu. To my surprise, Nancy orders it. I feel free to order it too. It is delicious.

Carla is here. After a tiny hint of awkwardness, we fall into each others' arms and cry.

"I'm free, I own the safari lodge, well you know, I can pay you back. I can never thank you enough. It looked as if I wouldn't get it. I was panicking. I was so afraid. I'm so sorry, Holly, I have been so stupid, I should have kept in touch with you. But I thought I might loose everything, and then what would you have thought of me? You would have thought I was trying to steal your money."

"I never thought badly of you, Carla. I trusted you."

"I'm so sorry," she said again. "You made this possible."

"Let's not talk about it again. Ever. It's all working out. Is there anything else I should know? Any romantic interest?"

"You mean my sex life? Darling! Nothing, as usual."

"Thing is, I know someone you'd love... he's called Figgy - I mean Lionel - only, just at the moment, he mustn't get over-excited - "

My mother is here.

"Darling, you'd love Zanzibar, the sea snakes were spectacular, and the turtles - !"

"For goodness sake, you haven't been diving?"

"No dear, I don't think they'd insure me at my age, just snorkelling. What fun!"

"So - mum - this is Steve."

"I remember you, you used to come round and take Holly out to play. You were a bit of a bad influence."

"Er - yes. I suppose that's what I want to do for the rest of my life. Be a bad influence on Holly."

She took me on one side.

"Darling."

"What?"

"Don't you think -?"

"What?"
"Well -"
"I don't believe this."
"What?"
"What are you trying to do?"
"What do you mean?"
"You're trying to undermine my relationship with Steve!"
"Not exactly..."
"What then?"
"You were brought home by the police once, because of that young man."

She was right, it was an episode I had managed to forget.

"But I was ten. We were ten."
"The age of criminal responsibility," she said reproachfully.
"It was mischief night."
"I think you'll find that would be ASBO night these days."
"Actually you do have a point. We used to put bangers through letter boxes."
"Precisely."
"That was then. This is now. You can't buy bangers any more."
"Well I just hope you know what you're doing," she said darkly.
"Honestly, mother, that's such a cliché!"
"Clichés contain important tHollys."
"Yes, yes, I know, but at crucial points in life it would be nice to have original thoughts."
"Maybe you're talking to the wrong person."
"Gosh, yes, mum - you're right! I should be talking to Steve!"

After dinner we all went back to Carla's, where we were staying for a few days. It was a short flight in a small plane away, and as we landed, we could see a man on the runway shooing away the baboons.

"They are so nosy!" said Carla. "Baboons! I don't know which is worse, the baboons or the hippos!"

We bumped to a halt on the grassy strip, and disembarked, if that's the right word.

"Oh, Carla!"

It was perfect. Perched on cliffs above the lazily flowing, crocodile and hippo infested river, the camp, with its bar and dining area overlooking a huge bend of the river and the mountains beyond, was like something out of a Child's Book of Africa. Carla tried to be modest, but failed.

"Oh, it is nothing, really. It is just another safari camp. I expect there are lots which are more luxurious. OK it is fabulous."

Suddenly: "Beep, beep!" went my phone.

"Who's sending you texts in Africa?" demanded Nancy, and Steve looked slightly worried. I looked at my phone.

"It's Naz, She says our programme's been on TV today. She said we looked lovely, Nance. Esp Nancy, she says."

"I hope I never have to watch it."

"She's made us a disk."

"Great."

"I want to see it," Steve began, but I gave him what I hoped was a warning look, and luckily it worked and he shut up. After a lovely supper (very Italian, gnocchi and a fabulous artichoke pasta dish - how odd in the African bush), we sat around the bar and got a bit tiddly. Nancy was on rum and coke, how like myself at her age, my mother was knocking back whisky in a way that reminded me, uncomfortably, of Roger, and Steve and I were sharing a bottle of Rioja. Carla was on her own supplies.

My mother was going on about Zanzibar and the turtles.

"I have never seen a creature which exudes such an air of wisdom, as a turtle," she said.

"They look as if they could tell you all the secrets of the universe."

"If only you could speak turtle," said Nancy.

"Don't be silly dear."

Carla's barman, after a warning look from Carla, reminded us all that we had a busy day ahead of us, an early start to drive out in the jeep to our wild camp, and with that he pointedly closed the bar and turned out the lights.

We stumbled back to our tents. Nancy was sharing with her grandmother, and she gave me a very dirty look as she went in, zipping up the flap in an extremely disgruntled manner.

"Don't worry about her," Steve said, taking me in his arms, when we were finally alone.

"She'll be fine. You worry too much about that girl."

"I know. I worry far too much. I'm over-protective."

"Is it to do with...?"

"Yes."

"You've never told me."

"No."

"Is it time?"

"Yes."

"Actually Nancy doesn't really know about it. I mean, she knows there was another baby. But not the details."

"Tell me whatever you want to."

"I want to tell you everything."

I couldn't speak.

"You don't have to."

"No. I need to."

"When Nancy was a baby. Ten months old. I got pregnant again. We wanted a family, you know, not just one. We were so happy. Nancy was a perfect baby, so good and happy. Just learning to walk. Chatty. And beautiful. But one, it didn't seem right, didn't feel like a whole family. And then I got pregnant. We were so excited about the new baby. Of course, she was too little to talk to about it. She never knew, then. I don't think so. I don't think she can have understood what happened."

"When I was seven months pregnant. We went out for a meal. To a country pub. Nancy was with a babysitter. She was fifteen months, then. She was talking properly. She said,

"Mummy, don't go out," because she was talking in proper sentences, and she cried. I had to leave her crying, I didn't want to go, because she was unhappy. My baby. But he said, don't let her rule your life like that. He said, she'll calm down. Don't spoil her. So we went out. I felt awful. I hated leaving her. She was so -, oh, I don't know. She was everything, my baby.

Then I remember I spent ages looking through the menu because there were so many things I wasn't allowed to eat. Soft cheese, and shellfish, and anything with alcohol in it, and rare meat. Chillies. We had a nice meal, I think, then we were driving home. He was driving. I should have been, but I was a bit too fat to get behind the wheel. It was dark. Late. Suddenly this car was there - in the road - headlights on full beam - it was a little narrow country road, we couldn't avoid him, we hit him full on. He hit us."

"We weren't really hurt. I mean, a bit of whiplash, that's all. It was the shock. It made me go into labour. They took me to hospital. I don't remember much about it, only sort of flashbacks, because they drugged me up, I think. It wasn't terribly early. I mean, seven months. He was born. He could have been OK. He should have been fine. I don't know what went wrong. It was a really bad time. Terribly bad. He was a boy. We called him Matthew. He was perfect. He was perfect. Couldn't have been more perfect. He died."

"That's awful."

"I know. But what was worse, was, we never talked about it. He would never talk to me about it. If I mentioned Matthew, he would say, there's no need to go over all that again, is there? We've dealt with that. Let's just move on, shall we?"

"Maybe he felt responsible?"

"Maybe."

"Was that where it all went wrong?"

"Maybe. I don't know. It's weird, I never thought about that before. Maybe it was. I was never allowed to talk about it. That's why it's so hard, now. I still feel as if I'm not allowed to talk about it."

"But you are."

We held each other tight, under our mosquito net, in the heart of Africa. The African night was all around us, throbbing. I felt as if I had emptied my bad dreams away, like pouring a bucket of fish into a river. I lay with my ear against Steve's chest, hearing the sound of his heart, beating with a steady, reliable rhythm. I felt safe, home, protected. I loved Steve. I loved Africa.

Suddenly, cutting violently into the peace of the night, there was a mighty crashing, nearby, as if someone had decided to cut all the trees down.

"What the hell?"

Steve got out of bed and cautiously unzipped part of the tent flap. He shone his torch into the blackness. Then he leapt back, zipping up the tent behind him. As if that would keep anything out.

"What is it?"

"An elephant, coming up from the river. Ripping branches off the trees."

"Oh no, oh God! Is it coming this way?"

"Shit, yes."

"We could go into the bathroom?"

The bathroom was attached to the tent, and happily was constructed of concrete. Unlike the tent, which was constructed of canvas. Of the flimsy sort.

"See what he does."

We unzipped the tent flap again, maybe six inches, and peered out. The elephant was still coming up the path. His ears were angrily flapping, his little eyes gleamed in the torchlight.

"Uh oh. He looks like Figgy," I said, almost getting the giggles.

He came towards us looking keen to trample all in his path, including any flimsy little tents which might have been carelessly left lying around. Just as I was about to retreat to the perceived shelter of the bathroom (I would fend him off with my toothbrush if necessary, I supposed), the elephant made a sharp turn to the right and trampled grumpily past, inches from our fragile flap. I peered into the night, anxious for Nancy (and my mother), but the elephant took no notice of any of our tents and kept going. All he wanted was leaves.

Steve and I went out into the moonlight. We listened until it was quiet again, apart from the hippos and the night birds and the insects, which actually weren't all that quiet. "There we go," he said. "All that crashing about is over now. Now we can get some peace. That's the end of all that. Let's go to bed."